The Art of Being a Patient
Taming Medicine – An Insider's Guide

The Art of Being a Patient
Taming Medicine – An Insider's Guide

Become a Proactive Partner and Self-Advocate of Your Own Health by Understanding Your Basic Rights and Privileges

By

Philip Caravella, M.D., F.A.A.F.P.

1stBooks – rev. 09/20/00

About the Book

The Art of Being a Patient
Taming Medicine – An Insider's Guide

This book educates patients about the internal workings of the health care system, to improve their chances of receiving world-class care by encouraging their participation as a proactive partner, self-advocate, and principle member of their health care team.

Problems with the delivery of health care have existed since the beginning of formal medical practice. Mistakes and errors of omission remain a growing problem as the delivery of medical care becomes more complex. The advent of managed care, initially touted as an answer, has, in the interest of saving money, added additional regulations to an already confusing arrangement. A lack of knowledge on the part of patients accounts for many of the problems they experience. On the other hand, the workings of the system often fail physicians as well, as they attempt to deliver quality health care. With better planning and preparation for medical office visits, patients can improve their chances of success dramatically. This book will assist those patients who feel they are on the outside looking in. It will even help those who understand the system and still manage to fall through the cracks. By providing a step-by-step guide to each office visit, this book promotes careful preparation, direct patient involvement, proper follow-through, and correct use of medication and preventive health practices.

Acknowledgements

My father, Louis, was a PFC in the Army, and my mother, Adele, was a homemaker. They moved with their twin children Philip and Phyllis to a "project" in Lakewood, Ohio, which was established for veterans and their families to begin a new life after World War II. While we lived for several years in homes that were converted barracks, my father and mother saved enough money to build a new home in Rocky River, a suburb of Cleveland, Ohio, in 1950. They chose Rocky River because in their research they had discovered that the Rocky River Public School System produced one of the highest percentages of student graduates to go on and attend colleges and universities. I wish to acknowledge the wisdom of their choice, for this school system remains a leader in public education in the area, receiving the highest academic accolades possible.

It is fitting to remember my early grade school teachers, who provided the building blocks without which I could not have succeeded. Next, I wish to remember the finest example of a teacher I have ever known, David Bichsel, a gifted high school civics and biology teacher. Also, I shall not forget Charles Shelton, an English teacher who taught me how to write creatively.

At the University of Dayton, Dr. Carl Michaelis, a professor of chemistry and mentor for premed students, first influenced me to enter the field of medicine. At Saint Louis University School of Medicine I served under Dr. Vallee Willman, the Chief of Surgery and the most professional physician I have ever encountered. During my first clinical rotation the summer of 1968, I worked alongside Dr. James Ottolini, Chief Resident in Obstetrics and Gynecology at St. John's Mercy Hosptial near St. Louis, Missouri. He influenced me more than anyone else in the concept of functioning as a team player in providing good health care. In 1970, at The Cleveland Clinic Foundation, I had the good fortune of working side-by-side with a fascinating physician, Dr. James Hewlitt, on his hematology-oncology service where our team performed one of the first bone marrow transplants in the Midwest. He taught me how delve deeply into possible causes of illness, and to never give up the search for a solution. I shall not forget Dr. Fred White at the University of Illinois, Peoria School of Medicine, where I served as Chief Resident in Family Medicine in the 1974-1975 academic year. He was the greatest all around physician I have ever encountered. Working in a small town outside of Peoria, he was the sine qua non of family physicians if there ever was one. His example and leadership has had the greatest influence on my life-long career as a family physician.

In the field of family medicine education there is no one more impressive to me than is Dr. Jack H. Medalie. Dr. Medalie is the finest educator in the field of family medicine that I have had the honor to work with and has been my friend and mentor for over twenty years. I owe him my gratitude for writing the forward to this book and for the lessons he taught to me during my postgraduate fellowship at Case Western Reserve University School of Medicine.

There are many individuals I wish to thank who graciously gave of their time during the writing and editing of my book. First I want to thank my son Phil, who typed the original manuscript from dictated notes. His efforts dramatically reduced the time necessary to bring this book into fruition. Next I wish to thank my daughter Kimberly and photographer and artist, Alan Tang. Kim posed as a model for Alan, who photographed her for use in promotional materials sent to numerous publishers for their consideration. He also shot the photograph of Kimberly used on the front cover of this book. My daughter Suzanne, also a gifted artist, is acknowledged for her assistance in cover design. Karen, my wife of 32 years, deserves a lot of credit, as an author widow, being deserted for about 1700 hours during the four years this book took to write.

I wish to remember the following individuals who reviewed the manuscript and offered numerous suggestions on how to improve the work: George and Carol Halter, Robert and Audrey Kreckle, Dennis Lekan,Ph.D., Sherry Lekan, and Jennifer Helland. They all deserve my sincere gratitude.

I wish to thank my editor, Vivian Wagner, Ph.D., and writer for *The Plain Dealer*, who turned my manuscript into an organized and reader friendly health related book . Lastly, I wish to thank Elizabeth Petrus and Karen Caravella, both of whom did a fine job in reviewing the final text for grammatical errors.

Dedication

To the sick and less fortunate who have not found refuge in the field of medicine despite the best intentions of all professionals who have been involved in their health care.

And

To my wife, Karen, and children, Philip, Kimberly, and Suzanne, who have provided for me the fullest meaning of life.

xii

Table of Contents

Preface

Over the nearly three decades I have been a physician as well as an educator, I remain chagrined at how often preventable problems occur during the delivery and reception of health care. The fault lies both with the medical profession and with the patients.

I'm sure that problems with the delivery of health care have existed since the beginning of formal medical practice. Mistakes and errors of omission remain a growing problem as the delivery of medical care becomes more complex. The advent of managed care in the interest of saving money has added additional regulations to an already confusing arrangement. On the one hand, a lack of knowledge on the part of patients who use the health care system accounts for many of the problems they experience. On the other hand, the workings of the system often also fail physicians in their attempts to deliver quality care.

None of us are immune – whether we be physicians or patients – from the unexpected pitfalls associated with the delivery of health care. With better planning and preparation, we can improve our chances of success in order to receive world-class care.

In an effort to help resolve many of the complex issues concerning modern medical care, I felt a detailed text on this subject would have value for those patients who feel they are on the outside looking in. This book will even help those who understand the system and yet still manage to fall through the cracks. One last goal of his book will be to convince those of you who have tended to be passive patients to become proactive partners.

Foreword

By Jack H. Medalie, M.D., M.P.H., F.A.A.F.P.,
The Dorothy Jones Weatherhead Professor Emeritus of
Medicine,
Case Western Reserve University

I approached this book with some misgivings – a physician writing about the art of being a patient!! Was this a physician being arrogant, or was this an honest attempt to identify with patients' problems? To my very pleasant surprise, I found that Dr. Caravella regards patients and physicians as partners, or, using his own analogy, the patient is the Captain of the ship and the doctor is the Navigator steering the ship in the right direction. Thus, everything Dr. Caravella discusses is with the intention of helping the patient, and indirectly the physician, to traverse the intricacies and obstacles of our multifaceted, complex, and often-chaotic health system.

Dr. Caravella presents the issues, the encounters, and the procedures in a very honest and direct way, emphasizing the importance of the patient's role in the patient-doctor relationship. He stresses, too, the importance (often lost in our hospital-oriented system) of prevention of disease and maintenance of health.

Interestingly, although the book is written basically for patients, there is a great deal that physicians and other health workers can learn from it and frankly, it would be helpful if medical insurance workers and health administrators would have this book on their required reading list.

It is my pleasure to recommend this book.

Disclaimer

Medical knowledge, diagnostic techniques, and treatment strategies, while generally improving, are in a constant state of flux. Though every effort has been made to ensure accuracy and to offer the best guidance, one should consult a physician before making any medical decisions.

The policies set forth within your health insurance plan may vary significantly from what is discussed in this manual. For financial reasons, you must become intimately familiar with all aspects of your own health plan and follow its recommendations as directed.

SECTION 1: PRELIMINARY ISSUES

Chapter 1

Working with the Health Care Industry

Patient frustration, uncaring physicians, and intolerable waits are the most often cited reasons for discontent within the doctor-patient health care relationship. These are valid complaints, but they represent only a few of the problems facing patients.

The following example helps to illustrate some of the most common problems in the delivery of quality health care to patients. At 7:00 a.m. one Saturday morning, Linda Jenkins, suffering from severe abdominal pain and fearing appendicitis, called her childhood family doctor – whom she hadn't seen in years. He directed her to a local emergency room. Linda, a 31-year-old patient, had been diagnosed six months earlier with a form of arthritis, but she was taking her medication only sporadically. Since she had recently started a new job, she had missed a follow-up office visit with her specialist and had also failed to reschedule the appointment. In addition, Linda had not taken time to familiarize herself with her new company's health insurance plan.

After being admitted to the emergency room, she was asked to list her medications, but she could not recall any of them. Linda also could not adequately describe her symptoms. Since she was unfamiliar with how to present a medical problem, she could only provide a vague account of her discomfort. She had not seen a physician in years for a PAP test, and she was very uncomfortable with medical care in general. Lacking important information, the emergency room doctor ordered numerous tests and x-rays to assist in his diagnosis. The evaluation required four hours and added up to a tidy sum of money. Fortunately, the emergency room doctor reassured her that she did not have appendicitis. Unfortunately, the cause of her problem remained undiagnosed. Linda was sent home with a recommendation to see her primary care physician within two or three days.

Due to the unfriendliness of our health care system and Linda's lack of knowledge, she was unwittingly involved in a

3

long list of errors and mishaps that cost her $1,523.50, and to say nothing of the anger and resentment the incident caused her to have for the medical profession and the health care industry. None of this had to happen – not even the abdominal pain.

With foresight and planning, Linda could have avoided the following errors:

1) Not recording or remembering the diagnosis of systemic lupus erythematosus – a joint and organ disease – six months earlier.
2) Not recording or remembering two medications with difficult generic names that had been prescribed to her.
3) Not taking medication as prescribed.
4) Not having thorough knowledge of her health insurance plan.
5) Not seeing her specialist in a follow-up visit after the initial diagnosis.
6) Not rescheduling the missed appointment.
7) Not making her first appointment with a primary care physician (PCP) before a crisis occurred.
8) Not calling the correct physician (one approved by her managed care plan) for permission to go to an emergency room.
9) Not visiting an emergency room that was on contract with her health plan.
10) Not having had routine care, which decreased her knowledge of how the health care industry operates.

Now Linda is faced with the following problems:

1) The fact that she is not yet established with her primary care physician complicates post-emergency room follow-up care.
2) Since she has never seen her primary care physician, Linda is technically not one of his/her patients.

4

3) Since she is not the patient of a primary care physician, he or she has no medical or legal obligation to provide follow-up care for her.
4) Linda is responsible for all of the costs incurred by her emergency room visit.

Hopefully, after reading this book and following its recommendations, you will not be as likely to fall into the traps and misfortunes that confronted Linda.

There comes a time when some issues vital to the public interest have been ignored for so long that they beg to be addressed. The doctor-patient relationship, as well as the patient-insurance company-doctor triad, are two neglected areas that have demanded attention for a long time. It is intended that this book speak to a large group of people – to provide insight and data regarding health care relationships that all of us will sooner or later experience. An attempt is made to look at problems from a patient's perspective, and to provide methods to address confusing or irritating issues that confront individuals when dealing with the health care system. The book will discuss common problems that occur repeatedly – albeit unintentionally – yet never seem to be resolved.

Several categories of patients will especially benefit from this book's insight and methods. After reading this text, those of you who have rarely entered the health care system will be much better prepared to do so. Women, especially mothers and their children, will be aided with advice about how to work effectively with their physician. The elderly, too, will be more able to cope with the complexities of every day medical care. Those of you who are tired of sitting in waiting rooms and exam rooms will be given ideas about how to solve vexing issues of this sort. The confusion and issues revolving around generic drugs versus name brand drugs will be clarified. The selection of a first-class physician will be explored. Ways to effectively prepare for your office visit will be thoroughly detailed. We will look at the important difference between an allergic drug reaction versus a side effect. Confusion between these two different problems may result in success or failure in the management of your

5

medical problem and could even mean the difference between life and death. Your medical record and how to reveal its secrets will also be explored. These are only a few carefully covered topics in this book. Answers to these and many other thought-provoking questions will provide comfort and security for those who will inevitably deal with the health care system.

Are you prepared to help your physician help you? If so, this book will be a valuable guide and reference book for any patient hoping to achieve high-quality health care without skipping a beat. When it comes to working with the health care industry nearly every patient struggles. This struggle is based partially on fear of the unknown, and partially on a lack of understanding of how the health care industry operates. Complicating the problem is the fact that some physicians lack the people skills necessary to deal effectively with their patients; they may consider themselves primarily scientists or researchers. Some physicians lack the social graces and warmth that typify professionals in the social services and religious ministries. As a result, they may appear cold, indifferent, aloof, or uncaring. In addition, many physicians are poor businessmen, unable to efficiently operate a medical office. This lack of sophistication sometimes shows itself by the employment of office personnel who are deficient in appropriate phone skills and people skills.

To further aggravate the situation, the managed care industry has reduced per-visit reimbursement and has instituted complex rules and regulations associated with prescription medications, referrals, and testing. To cover increasing costs, physicians have been forced to see more patients, shuffle more paperwork, and deal with many more business-related problems than ever before. This has led to crowded office schedules, long waits, and often dissatisfaction for patients well before they even see their physician.

Managed care programs usually require physicians on their panel to accept new patients who have chosen them – even when their practices are full or overloaded. This overflow can reach epic proportions during the winter months, when the flu season and infectious diseases are rampant. Patients often fail to visit with their new physician under serene circumstances; instead,

6

they procrastinate until a crisis and then hope to be served by an already busy medical practice. When a new patient calls his or her physician's office for the first time – hoping to be seen that day for treatment of an acute problem – they may be disappointed. Often they will be told that their doctor's first available new patient appointment is one or two months down the road. Unfortunately, after hearing that troubling response, they have already gotten off on the wrong foot long before meeting their new primary care physician.

This is only the beginning of many problems that can and will occur if you are not prepared to deal with the complexities of receiving medical care. People expect their medical institutions to provide excellent care. A large multi-specialty health care center like The Cleveland Clinic Foundation, for instance, is proud of its role in providing the best of care to its diverse international patient population. With an emphasis on the latest in research and technology, The Cleveland Clinic provides "world class care" to its patients. Yet due to the complexities and nature of the business, such quality care does not happen by chance. The good news, however, is that world-class medical care is available to all who learn what is necessary to receive it. If you diligently follow the guidelines in this book, you will be in a better position to receive good, comprehensive health care.

This may sound like wishful thinking, but it is not. Like everything else in life, those who are well-prepared and well-organized will be successful in reaching their goals despite the disorganization inherent in the world around them. Being a good patient is an art form. You must attempt to understand the health care industry in order to be better prepared to work with your physician, to solve problems, and to receive good results. Few books describe the pitfalls of the health care system, and even fewer demonstrate how to fix the problems and successfully traverse the obstacle course of managed care. As you read, you will be provided with insight, methods and answers that will help you to receive the world-class health care you deserve.

7

Chapter 2

Who's Captain of the Ship?

The single most important challenge facing the health care industry is communication. Patients are provided with information from many sources, but they often find it difficult to sort through this information. The doctor-patient relationship is the key to a successful journey through the complicated, often confusing maze of the health care delivery system. Not too long ago, patients were told what to do. Now, since they are better-informed and educated through television and the Internet, some patients are even a little ahead of their physicians. Because of these changes, patients now need to be partners in their own care, and they must be involved in the decision-making process. Yet no matter how informed they feel, they still require their physician to review their decisions and to provide appropriate guidance and management.

A patient of mine, Janet Schrott, wrote a few comments to me when she learned of this book. She said that "a patient needs to be receptive to the doctor's suggestions, ask questions and be sure they understand what the doctor is trying to communicate. They also need to be informed through other techniques, like reading, attending seminars, etc. The basis of the art of being a patient is trust in yourself and those who can help you. So there needs to be a partnership developed. The doctor, as well, needs to be open to what the patient is saying." Janet clearly recognizes the need for mutual understanding and support within the framework of the doctor-patient relationship.

Research indicates that there is an unintentional conspiracy of silence encompassing the doctor-patient relationship. Deborah L. Roter, a professor from Johns Hopkins School of Hygiene and Public Health, has said that "patients don't ask and doctors don't tell." Doctors have been trained to give orders rather than discuss knowledge – a tendency which makes many people uncomfortable in their dealings with the health care system.

In the final analysis, you must find a physician you trust and with whom you are comfortable. Your family physician must be your friend, confidant and teacher. At the same time, you must be open-minded, inquisitive and cooperative. The more you know and understand, the more sense your treatment will make and the more likely you will be to follow through with your treatment. Lack of knowledge results in uneasiness, distrust, and even sometimes the belief that the medical profession is incompetent, money-oriented or uncaring.

We can liken the doctor-patient relationship to that of a ship's captain and its navigator. The ship's captain is in charge of the vessel. He is ultimately responsible for whatever happens to his ship and its crew, good, bad, or otherwise. The navigator is an advisor. He charts the best, safest and most expedient course to follow. The captain need not heed the navigator's advice, and sometimes – during unusual circumstances – he may even override the navigator's recommendations. In a doctor-patient relationship, the patient is in the role of the captain, and the physician is in the role of the navigator. Your physician is an advisor and an expert in that role. Overriding your physician's directions – by refusing certain examinations or tests, not taking medications correctly, failing to follow up as advised, failing to see consultants, and so on – will eventually result in a shipwreck. A captain who repeatedly fails to take good advice will soon be a captain of a dangerous (sick) or incompetent vessel (body). Research strongly indicates that when patients take an active and positive role in their health care, they have the best outcomes.

Chapter 3

The Art of Being a Patient

He who is afraid to ask is ashamed of learning.
-- **Danish Proverb**

Art requires skill and perception – perhaps even more than science. Whereas science describes reality in the way it exists, art is richer and more meaningful, transcending facts and statistics. The art of being a good patient goes beyond medical science; it requires personal involvement every step of the way. To achieve and maintain good health, you must look beyond what *appears* to be acceptable, because it often is not.

Receiving world-class health care for yourself and your family requires a great degree of patient involvement. Better preparation prior to your medical office visits will go a long way in reducing or preventing the problems. Relying less on chance, some on intuition, and most heavily on knowledge will allow interested patients to understand the workings of the health care system. The health care system has not intentionally withheld secrets. It has simply assumed too much and has taken on too much responsibility. It is time for well-informed patients to regain control over their destiny, and this can be achieved through careful planning, awareness and action.

Women have done more to foster good medical care than anybody else. They make up almost 46% of the work force, they are the main health care decision makers and they are health care's primary consumers. Women will more often than not take the initiative in receiving routine health care, since often they feel a responsibility not only to themselves, but also to their family. In contrast to women, men are often at the other end of the spectrum. Barbara Watkins, a 47-year-old housewife, commented to me once, "If I didn't schedule the appointment for Jack he would never come in. He hates doctors. He always says he's just fine. What does he need to see a doctor for?" Men often do not participate as closely as women in general health

11

care needs; they tend to let things slide, focusing on other family responsibilities and leaving health care decisions up to the women in their lives.

For a variety of reasons, many people fail to seek any form of health care for years or even decades at a time. Some feel so healthy, they believe it is unnecessary. These people overlook the fact that they may carry genetic disorders, or that their health is impacted upon by environmental factors – such as severe work stress – which if left unattended to will eventually take a toll. Others need help in dealing with smoking, high cholesterol, high blood pressure and other insidious silent killers.

Then there are those fearful, paranoid adults who have known friends or relatives who have suffered adverse consequences through their dealings with the health care system. Everyone seems to have a story to tell about someone else's health care misadventure. "I remember Bill," they will say. "Once they found out he had cancer, his real problems began." These people may remain aloof from the health care system, fearing similar negative results could befall them. With good care, however, most patients do well in today's medical arena. Comparing your personal medical problems to those of others is often misleading and may delay effective treatment.

Finally, another large group of people live in fear of what a physician may find. This syndrome, a form of *blinded euphoria*, relies on the misconception that if one doesn't look for something wrong, it isn't there. This syndrome is surprisingly ubiquitous, tending to afflict many patients in their 40s and 50s. Such people will think, "Maybe there's something there, maybe not. I'm not going to look for trouble. If I mind my own business, I'll do just fine." Unfortunately, they are often correct in their fears. They err, however, in not realizing that if their health problems were treated, they could lead normal and fulfilling lives.

Good health care is a complicated and time-consuming adventure. There are many opportunities for mistakes, shortfalls and less-than-ideal outcomes. To reduce your chances of poor medical care, you must become a partner and active member of your health care team. Those who sit back and wait for things to happen are often lost, forgotten, or prematurely buried. With good planning, you will be more likely to benefit from all of the wonders of modern medical science. *Remember, the art of being a good patient requires that you fully participate as a patient. That is the need and the challenge.*

Chapter 4

Education and Credibility of Physicians

"You can get by on charm for about 15 minutes. After that, you better know something."
H. Jackson Brown, Jr.,
Live and Learn and Pass It On

To better understand the breadth of the problem, you need to understand how physicians are educated. Physicians are essentially scientists and researchers who must master countless scientific and medical principles. After becoming experts in the scientific realm of medicine, most physicians must learn the real art of medical care – the application of humanistic principles to the care of patients. Max DePree, in his book, Leadership Is an Art, has argued, that "Intimacy is at the heart of competence. It has to do with understanding, with believing and with practice." Outstanding physicians are able to develop a form of intimacy with their patients which combines their knowledge with a sense of caring. And while the best physicians master this combination, others never do.

The futility of self-diagnosis and illness management by a patient's friend or family becomes more apparent after one understands the content of medicine. Without comprehensive medical knowledge, extensive experience and deductive thinking, it is not possible to provide successful health care. That is why so many of the so-called health care providers who practice on the fringes of the system cannot usually provide comprehensive – or even acceptable – medical care. Although they may supplement what physicians have to offer, they simply do not have the level of training and knowledge that would allow them to replace physicians.

To begin with, most medical schools are highly selective in their search for excellence among students. Most medical students have already spent four years as undergraduate students;

15

some have achieved master's degrees and doctorates before beginning their four years of medical school. Even for the most informed, however, medical school remains a challenge. To begin, medicine requires a diverse curriculum. Freshman year concentrates on the disciplines of biochemistry, gross anatomy, histology and physiology. Later on, pharmacology, neural anatomy, psychology and pathology must be mastered. Eventually, students learn the art of physical examination and then progress into the fields of internal medicine, general surgery, obstetrics, gynecology, psychiatry, family medicine and several subspecialties. Preventive medicine concepts are learned in each area as their studies continue. During their four years of medical school, students must pass national medical board examinations.

After graduation from medical school, physicians then move into graduate studies in their chosen specialty. New physicians will spend an additional three to six years in post-graduate medical studies, attempting to master any one of two dozen or more possible specialties. After completing their specialty studies, they then must pass additional extensive board examinations before beginning their specialty and the practice of medicine. Throughout their careers, specialists have to repeat these exams every six to ten years to maintain their board certification status. Few, if any, professions require so much initial education, as well as so much ongoing, continuous education throughout a career.

The requirements of a well-rounded physician are summed up in the following quote, taken from an original article by Faith Fitzgerald, M.D. first published in the *'The Annals of Internal Medicine'* in 1996; 124 (1 pt 1): 71

WANTED: 21st Century Physician

Altruistic, compassionate, courageous, intellectually curious, frugal scholar, gifted in history, philosophy, politics, economics, sociology, and psychology. Must have working knowledge of biology, chemistry, physics, and medicine. Physical endurance, emotional maturity, and technical-manual skills sufficient to take apart and reassemble the human body and mind at levels ranging from the micro molecular to the gross are required; must have flexibility to master all knowledge, sift and discard that no longer applicable, while discovering new data at the bench, in clinical practice, in both general and subspecialty medicine. Teaching, counseling, administrative, computer and budgetary expertise essential, as is commitment to the disenfranchised. A working knowledge of the law; literary, artistic, and musical talent; and multilingualism highly desirable. Should be able to prevent and cure disease, including the depredations of advancing age; physical disarray; and spiritual, mental, emotional, and economic illnesses. Will need to function effectively and efficiently in both intensive care units and urban slums.

Salary ideally should be no issue, though heavy initial investment by the candidate is required. Benefits variable, depending on the individual's principal source of gratification. This is a 24-hour per day commitment.

Should make house calls.

In the end, patients must be skeptical when being counseled for health problems by someone other than a medical professional. The opinions of close and meaningful friends and neighbors may appear to be authoritative, but laymen cannot compete with the broad education of physicians. The complexity and diversity of human disease remains a challenge even for the most experienced and educated of physicians.

With knowledge and hard work, you can become an expert in your own personal medical problems. Patients who become advocates of their own health will be rewarded with better health and probably a longer and more vigorous life. Physicians and patients must work together in a cooperative arrangement to arrive at an effective and therapeutic program. Unfortunately, all plans – no matter how sensible and reasonable they appear – may break down in the course of delivery unless patients remain diligent in their efforts to achieve the best. Physicians cannot shoulder the responsibility alone. Every patient must have a clear understanding of what is expected. They must know how to traverse the inevitable potholes that will be encountered along the complex highway of health care delivery.

Chapter 5

Medical Insurance: An Option That is Not Optional

Our journey along the highway of good health begins with acquiring some form of adequate medical insurance. Without acceptable medical insurance, health care would be far too costly for the majority of people. Individuals lacking medical insurance use health care services less frequently and are less likely to accept preventive medicine as a way of life. When they do seek medical services, they are also less likely to fill expensive prescriptions. Not taking recommended medication will often result in further deterioration of their health. There is little point in seeing a physician if prescriptions are not filled and taken as prescribed.

Some form of medical insurance coverage is a must for those who wish to access the majority of health care services now available. In principle, everyone should have access to the best of what is available, but in practice, without insurance, many people would not have this access. Many people spend more time shopping for a television than they do investigating available options for medical insurance. The best and often the only place to start is to evaluate options available from your employer. Full-time employees are often offered some form of health insurance coverage. Some businesses currently offer several plans from which to choose. It may be worthwhile when comparing one plan to another to consider the differences in deductible expenses, copays and prescription costs that must be met each year.

If you're currently seeing a physician with whom you're comfortable, discussing your options for selecting health care plans might be a good idea. He or she will be able to discuss the general reputation of the plans, the ease (or lack thereof) in referrals to specialists, quality of drugs on the plans, and the reputations of physicians and hospitals associated with the plans.

The importance of having adequate health insurance coverage for yourself and your family cannot be overstated. It is even worth considering changing jobs in order to have access to some form of adequate medical coverage. It is true that health insurance is available to all who are willing to pay for it, but the cost is usually prohibitive without access to large group policies available primarily through the business community.

What about those of you who change jobs and have become insured by another policy at your new place of employment? Does your new plan cover preexisting conditions or problems that were being treated prior to you new job? The Kennedy-Kassebaum Health Care Bill of 1996 now provides for automatic coverage of preexisting problems through your new employer if the company offers insurance to its employees.

Health Insurance Plans: A Few Options

Not too many years ago, most of us were covered under fee-for-service medical insurance plans. Under these arrangements, a patient could go to any doctor or hospital she/he wanted to but would also be responsible for paying deductible expenses at the start of each new contract year. These expenses generally amounted to $100 to $200 per year, per family. After meeting deductibles, office visits were free or sometimes subject to a ten to twenty percent copayment due at time of services rendered. Your physician would then bill your insurance company for the balance due. Usually, whatever your physician billed was fully covered. If tests were ordered, they were paid for. All referrals to other physicians were reimbursable. Patients could choose their own physicians and specialists. When needed, patients could be admitted to hospitals of their choice.

This system resulted in a high degree of satisfaction for both patients and physicians, though it was not necessarily economical. Obvious abuses by some physicians led to overcharges, unnecessary testing and prolonged hospital stays. Although overcharges and over-utilization of medical services was not the standard of operation for most physicians, enough abuses occurred – resulting in skyrocketing costs. This situation

20

eventually forced insurance companies to take another look at reimbursement practices. Eventually, companies developed new insurance plans and controlled their policies more tightly – all but eliminating the influence of physicians and institutions.

Fee-for-service plans still exist, but they are much more restricted than they once were. Since they are the most expensive option, they are rarely available as a choice for most patients through their place of employment. Even executives rarely have this option within the current medical insurance climate.

Among the common health insurance options are managed care plans, many of which were born on the west coast. The Kaiser Foundation began decades ago as one of the earliest examples of managed care, and it continues today to have a large share of the market. Simply put, managed care is a form of closely-controlled medical care, reducing options to only a few choices. Reducing choices results in lower cost. In most managed care plans, patients are only allowed to see specific physicians and hospitals that are under contract. Physicians are also limited in the choices of medications that they are permitted to prescribe for their patients, except under special or unusual circumstances.

Managed care insurance companies contract with all branches of the health care industry to obtain the lowest fees for office visits, hospital stays and laboratory testing. They negotiate contracts with national pharmaceutical firms to provide for discounted generic and proprietary medications. One of the difficult problems facing physicians is that they must try to prescribe only those medications that are listed on a patient's list of approved drugs. This list of approved medications is referred to as the insurance company's formulary, and it varies significantly with each health plan.

Some of the changes brought on by managed care have benefited the consumer. Competition for the health care dollar by all factions of the health care industry, for example, has resulted in less costly testing. There are also constant attempts at all levels of the industry to improve performance without sacrificing quality.

No system is ideal, however, and there have been cases of abuse by physicians and hospitals. One form of abuse is the use of incorrect coding procedures by medical care providers when billing for services rendered. Some unscrupulous providers have been known to charge for services never provided. They have also charged for higher levels of care then were actually provided to the patient. These unacceptable practices can escalate costs for everyone.

Another form of abuse, however, is the overzealous restrictions by insurance companies that may compromise one's choices and severely limit the duration of hospital stays. As an example, a few years ago most of us were familiar with postpartum hospital stays that were so brief they were referred to by some as drive-through deliveries. New and forthcoming legislation has reduced some of these obvious abuses. For example, U.S. District Judge Vanessa Gilmore upheld a Texas law in September of 1998, allowing consumers to sue health insurers when insurance company decisions resulted in injury, death or economic loss.

Modern medical science has developed wonderful new diagnostic procedures that many of us are familiar with, such as CAT scans and MRIs. They are quite useful, but they remain very expensive. By saving money in some areas, health care organizations have freed up dollars to be used for newer diagnostic studies that would otherwise not be financially feasible. There will always be cost constraints limiting the use of new technology. Contemporary testing and surgical procedures, however, will remain available to most individuals who need them. Although access to medical care often appears limited, few nations enjoy a health care system that is as advanced as ours and yet remains available to such a diverse population base.

The two most common forms of managed care plans include Health Maintenance Organizations (HMOs) and Preferred Provider Organizations (PPOs). There are several other examples of health care networks that are less common or are variations of the above and will not be reviewed.

HMOs provide to their enrollees lists of physicians, hospitals and other facilities from which patients must choose. Usually services are covered based on a fixed payment schedule that all parties have agreed to in advance. The cost of medical insurance is usually covered by one's employer or by enrollees themselves. Often an enrollee is subject to a $5 to $10 copayment, which is due at time of services rendered. The exact amount of one's copay will vary from plan to plan. There is a trend to raise copays to help defray unexpected costs that are creeping into the health care arena. One way or another costs will be born by the benefactors.

Analysts believe HMOs will endure since they have been effective in controlling rising costs. Paul Ginsburg, President for the Center for Studying Health System Change in Washington, D.C., believes that, "Even though HMO's receive a lot of criticism about their practices, no one is going to take their place." There doesn't appear to be any alternative health insurance systems currently available that can perform better financially or more efficiently than current HMO systems. Granted there is always room for improvement with any business and changes are forth coming.

In November, 1999, United Health Group (UHG), an HMO, decided it would let physicians, not administrators, make the final decisions on patient care. This is a refreshing change of policy and one that should improve relations between the UHG HMO, its enrollees, and its physician panel. It should be noted that UHG would likely release physicians who repeatedly order unnecessary tests or leave patients in hospitals for excessive lengths of stay.

It is of interest to note that only seven large HMO's are currently operating in most of the US. In recent years several HMO's have joined forces or have been assimilated to reduce expenses.

After a patient has chosen an HMO or similar health care plan they must than begin the process of selecting a primary care physician, or PCP, from their plan's panel of experts to provide for their medical care and that of their family. Under most HMO plans, your primary care physician, or gatekeeper, controls referrals to specialists, hospitals and participating facilities. When the time comes your PCP will determine the frequency and number of visits that you are allowed for each specialist. Your PCP after referring you to a specialist will frequently have to approve expensive tests or procedures recommended by the specialist before they can be carried out.

After reviewing the results of a specialist's consultation, your physician will then decide if he feels comfortable in carrying out the recommended treatment plan as suggested by the consultant. If he is comfortable with administering the treatment plan, he may decide to continue. If not, your PCP will ask the specialist to manage your medical problems – at least for the time being. Over time, referrals to specialists will expire and can only be renewed by your PCP if you wish to have the cost of future visits covered by your health plan.

Many patients tend to use emergency rooms incorrectly – at least from the point of view of their health care plans. Sick individuals who find it difficult to arrange for an appointment with their physician either due to a lack of appointment slots or inconvenient hours may be tempted to overuse emergency rooms for non-emergency problems. Under most managed care plans, patients must seek pre-approval before an emergency room visit, regardless of the time of day their problem has occurred. Failure to do so will often lead to a lack of reimbursement.

Life-threatening emergencies fall into a different category and are handled differently by insurance companies. Some medical policies only pay for true emergencies. If your "emergency" did not turn out to be one, some plans will refuse to cover the cost. According to Martin Gottlieb in his book, *The Confused Consumer's Guide to Choosing a Health Care Plan*, "Legislative efforts in many states require plans to pay for care that a *prudent layman* would identify as an emergency, regardless of the outcome." Obviously, insured patients should not be responsible for expensive medical services when serious emergencies occur and there is no time to contact your health plan to seek advanced approval. A few catastrophes that require immediate attention, whether or not the nearest emergency room is part of your health plan, include unexplained chest pain, serious burns, breathing problems and loss of consciousness. In a dire emergency, you should promptly proceed to the nearest emergency room for immediate care, without worrying about your health care plan. After hospitalization and emergency treatment has been rendered, most insurance carriers will require that they be contacted within a twenty-four to forty-eight hour time frame to obtain approval for the emergency visit. After your emergency has been satisfactorily managed and you are considered stable, your PCP must decide if continued care in the hospital remains necessary. If continued hospital care is necessary, your physician must also determine whether or not to allow an extended stay at the hospital to which you were first admitted. To save money, your PCP may decide to transfer you to a hospital that has contracted with your health care plan. These arrangements can vary, depending on your condition and the policies of your HMO.

Health plan enrollees who choose to see a physician without a referral from their PCP often will be responsible for whatever costs may be incurred. Self-referral is a frequent error on the part of many patients. Few, if any, HMO plans allow for self-referrals, because that arrangement would defeat the primary goal of the plans – to make a profit for its stock holders by controlling health care costs. This is why the current health care system for the majority of us is referred to as managed care. The point to remember is that they manage our care; we do not. In Washington a consumer rights bill is being haggled over by the senate and house that would expand consumers' opportunities to sue HMOs. This will not be the boon it appears to be, since the higher costs associated with litigation would ultimately be passed on to the consumer. After all, there is no such thing as a free lunch, as some people would like to believe.

Many patients are used to selecting their own doctors or visiting specialists they have seen before. Physician gatekeepers are sometimes given leeway after the fact in approving these misguided visits. PCPs who are considered too liberal in approving inappropriate referrals may not be enrolled as a provider again, when their contract year expires. Losing your family doctor in this fashion presents another whole new set of problems.

Another common form of a managed care organization is a Preferred Provider Organization, or PPO. PPOs are groups of physicians who join forces with insurance companies, hospitals, and employers to provide care at discounted rates for employees or members of specific groups. Patient members of PPOs can use physicians or facilities outside of their plan, but must pay additional fees of twenty to forty percent to cover expenses beyond the discounted rate.

There are many variations of these plans, but all will result in extra charges or financial risk when patients go outside of their network either by choice or by mistake. Patients are always required to understand the terms of their health insurance contracts. Simply going to convenient hospitals or familiar physicians that are not within your health care network will usually result in stiff financial penalties or no coverage at all. It is also important to remember that members of PPOs scheduled for hospital admission require advance approval or precertification arranged by their physician.

Certain types of services that patients received *free* in the past, when insured by fee-for-service contracts, may or may not be covered under some managed care plans. For example, some patients frequent their physician for an annual physical exam. A few are quite disappointed when they discover that some services such as routine annual physical exams may no longer be covered. If you are unsure about whether or not a specific service such as a physical exam is covered under your health plan, always call your insurance carrier before scheduling an appointment. In this manner you will know in advance what charges, if any, may be incurred.

Some patients who wish to have their insurance plan reimburse them for a routine physical exam request that their physician alter service codes used for insurance billing to reflect symptoms or diseases rather than routine preventive health care. Marianne Hardy, an expert in medical insurance policies and their rules and regulations, cautions patients, "Please remember the physician cannot code your claim for better reimbursement.

The insurance carrier considers this fraud. Your physician will attach the diagnosis which he or she feels is most accurate to describe the reason for your visit." False Claims Act 31 USC Sec. 3729, states that "Any Person who knowingly presents a false claim for payment is liable to the United States Government for a civil penalty of not less than $5,000 and not more than $10,000 plus 3 times the amount of damages...and no proof of specific intent to defraud is required." Also Medicare Special Bulletin B-89-23 notes, "Medicare law states that claims submitted which do not include the required codes will be denied. A civil money penalty and sanction is possible for any physician who knowingly, willfully, and in repeated cases fails to provide the required codes."

Preventive care is rarely a covered service with traditional indemnity coverage. Preventive care is often, however, covered by HMO plans. Usually for female patients a PAP test and a mammogram is paid for on an annual basis. This, however, may really mean that the cytology or actual lab test is covered, but not the office visit required to obtain the specimen. For most HMO plans preventive care is a covered benefit. If in doubt about what your plan covers, make sure to check it out before you make an appointment.

The more fully patients understand the rules and regulations established by their health care plan, the fewer disputes that will arise between them, their health care providers and their insurance companies. Forewarned is forearmed, as the old saying goes. Good care is available within most managed care plans when one understands how to access it and how to play by the rules. When it comes to money issues, mistakes are not easily forgiven nor rebated. Please see appendix G for a review on how to avoid medical insurance billing problems and what to do about billing and payment problems you may be facing.

There are some forms of illness and injury that may not fall directly under the guidelines of your medical insurance. Injuries that occur at work, or those related to your occupation, may fall under workman's compensation and must be reported to your employer. Likewise, when scheduling an office visit with your physician for a work-related disorder, be sure to mention this important fact to the appointment secretary. Not all physicians deal with workman's compensation, and you may have to be referred elsewhere. Once again, problems are avoidable when all parties fully understand the situation.

Injuries related to automobile accidents that may be the fault of someone else is another area where coverage may vary. Medical expenses may have to be borne by the party or parties that caused the accident. Checking with your insurance company when the situation allows may avoid later reimbursement problems.

In summary, all insured patients must be familiar with their insurance policy to avoid problems. Know which hospitals you can go to. Know which physicians you can see. Try to become as familiar with your insurance plan as possible. Since your plan was designed to meet the needs of your place of employment, it will vary from all other plans. When necessary, check with your workplace to clarify issues not fully explained by your insurance handbook. Ignorance of the details of your health plan is not an acceptable defense, as far as your health insurance company is concerned, and it may result in unnecessary costs to you. Take the initiative and learn about all aspects of your health insurance coverage. It will pay off in many ways. You may even discover extra benefits you didn't realize you had.

Most important of all, develop a strong and honest relationship with your physician. Traversing the minefield of managed care is tricky at best. Allowing your physician an opportunity to get to know you and your family well will endear him to your needs so that he will more readily go to bat for you when the occasion demands it.

Should You Ever Let Health Insurance Lapse?

The short answer is "no." Try never to allow your medical insurance to lapse. If you leave a company where medical coverage has been available, it is important to continue your medical insurance until you find a new job that provides coverage. You may be able to extend your current coverage for several months after you leave your job. This arrangement can function as a bridge until medical insurance with your new job kicks in. It is also usually payable through a monthly premium. Be sure to take advantage of this option if it is available to you. Even after finding a new job, there is usually a period of one to three months before your new policy is in force, should one be available at all. I have seen many patients during their job hiatus fail to carry short-term medical insurance and then wind up in dire financial states when a medical crisis occurs. The extra coverage is not cheap, but it is worthwhile in the case of emergencies which by definition are rarely predictable.

Before leaving your job, you may be able to negotiate short-term medical coverage as part of a separation agreement. If this does not work, contact your family insurance agent, who may be aware of some form of temporary medical insurance coverage until you have become established in a new job with benefits. If lack of money is a problem, you might want to consider borrowing money from a friend or relative to help maintain some form of coverage. Finding or funding first class medical care without insurance can be a trying experience.

SECTION II: CHOOSING A DOCTOR

Chapter 6

Primary Care Physicians: How Come?

Prior to the age of health maintenance organizations, patients were fairly free to see who they wished for medical services. A patient would begin by trying to analyze their symptoms, arrive at some form of a diagnosis and then select a specialist to visit for medical evaluation and therapy. For example, a woman experiencing abdominal pain might have decided to see a gynecologist for help. Or she might instead have gone to see a general surgeon, or a gastroenterologist. Or she might have chosen her family physician. Or, fearing the worst, she might have gone to see an oncologist right from the start – especially if she knew a friend or relative who had recently been diagnosed with cancer. In fact, she might have visited several specialists before eventually finding the right one.

This process was expensive and time-consuming. Managed care insurance companies believed, and rightly so, that one should first see a primary care physician to initially evaluate his or her problem, and thus begin the process of diagnosis and treatment. In recent years, their policy has proven to be the correct path to follow. In fact, many experts believe that "the difference between a family physician and a specialist is that one treats what you have, while the other thinks you have what they treat" (unknown author). It's not uncommon for specialists lacking comprehensive background in general medical problems to order borderline or questionable tests. This is generally not the case, however, when patients are referred to a specialist by their primary care physician. Inappropriate referrals and unnecessary testing were much more commonplace when patients were left to their own devices.

The above issue brings to mind a recent incident that occurred in October, 1999. Elaine C., a 63- year-old woman and long-time patient of mine, went to visit a gastroenterologist. A gastroenterologist specializes in problems associated with the esophagus, stomach, small intestine and large bowel – also known as the colon. Having a family history of colon cancer, she required cancer screening through a procedure known as colonoscopy. With this procedure, a flexible scope is passed into the rectum to investigate the entire length of the large bowel, as the physician searches for evidence of colon cancer.

During her visit, the G.I. physician believed her skin to be thinner or more wrinkled than expected for her age. He also noticed a prominent fat pad over her upper spine near the base of her neck. This change is sometimes referred to in medical circles as a buffalo hump when associated with Cushing's Syndrome. Cushing's Syndrome is actually a group of disorders characterized by over production of hormones, primarily cortisol, which can lead to a multitude of unsatisfactory effects. Fearing that she may have a form of Cushing's syndrome, he recommended and ordered a number of tests totaling over $350.00. Knowing this patient quite well and having seen her regularly, I personally had never considered the possibility of Cushing's. Fortunately, her tests turned out to be normal. The gastroenterologist, attempting to evaluate for a condition beyond his usual level of expertise wasted money and put Elaine through unnecessary testing.

The lesson to be learned with this example is that it is best to talk to your PCP before undergoing tests recommended by a specialist outside of their usual field of expertise. Your PCP is best suited to decide when and how to proceed. If I had been uncertain about Elaine's condition, I would have referred her to an endocrinologist for evaluation. An endocrinologist is an expert in disorders such as Cushing's syndrome, diabetes, thyroid problems and other disorders of the endocrine system.

Another good example of the benefits of first seeing a PCP is the common problem of chronic severe headaches. Patients commonly attribute recurrent headaches to eye conditions or spectacle (corrective lenses) problems, when in fact there might be other causes for their headaches. For example, Vanessa O., a seventeen-year-old high school student, had been suffering from early morning recurrent headaches for months. Unable to put up with her problem any longer, she first sought the opinion of an eye specialist. "Most headaches are due to eye problems,"

Vanessa commented to her mother. This was her first mistake, since, in fact, recurrent headaches are seldom due to eye problems according to Dr. Louis P. Caravella, a noted Cleveland ophthalmologist. Dr. Caravella noted that one's eyes are rarely related to the cause of headaches unless their headaches are accompanied by eye pain, eye redness, or blurred vision. There is an exception involving a patient that frequently uses her eyesight for close up work. These patients may suffer from recurrent headaches, according to Dr. L. Caravella.

Not realizing these points, Vanessa revisited her optometrist, who had given her a prescription for new eyeglass lenses only months earlier. He found that her prescription was correct, so fearing some other more serious problem he referred her to a local ophthalmologist, or eye specialist, for a second opinion. The ophthalmologist also found her to have a normal eye exam.

After ruling her eyes out, Vanessa thought that maybe her headaches were sinus related. She then visited an ear, nose, and throat specialist – who also gave her a clean bill of health. Now she began to fear the worst – a brain tumor. She sought the expertise of a neurologist, who also put her through a series of tests and scans. Fortunately, her tests were normal, which put her worst fears to rest. This situation still left several other potential causes of recurrent headaches that could have explained Vanessa's problem. Her headaches may have also been due to allergies, arthritis, TMJ (temporal mandibular joint) Syndrome, classic migraines, atypical migraines, neurological diseases of various types, and several other causes beyond the scope of this book. Vanessa had been spending a lot of time and money seeing a lot of "specialists," but in the end she still had not determined the cause of her headaches.

As in the case of Vanessa, most recurrent headaches – especially when one awakens with them on a frequent basis – are due to spasm of neck and shoulder muscles. These muscle spasm headaches are often caused by stressful situations either at home or at work. Under stress, muscles in the back of the neck and shoulders will tug on a heavy membrane located around the base of the skull named the apaneurosa. This tugging effect often results in common muscle spasm headaches.

Diagnosing the cause of headaches can prove to be an exhausting and troublesome process if left to the layperson to sort out. A well-trained family practitioner or general internist is best suited to begin the initial evaluation and treatment. Narrowing down the possibilities and then referring quickly to the appropriate specialist when necessary can save a lot of pain, time and money. On most occasions, an experienced primary care physician can diagnose and treat headaches effectively within the framework of a single office visit.

Being well trained in the evaluation of the total patient, a PCP or family physician is best suited to jump-start the evaluation and treatment of most illnesses. Managed care insurance companies have realized the wisdom of this approach, which is why they now require patients to be evaluated initially by their PCP before investigating other options.

Chapter 7

Selecting a Family Physician vs. a General Internist or Pediatrician

After you have arranged for your medical insurance coverage, the next hurdle is to select a primary care physician (PCP). Not too many years ago, the process was fairly simple. You went to the general practitioner (GP) your folks went to. Increasing mobility, however, has led to frequent moves by most Americans, nearly eliminating the traditional practice of seeing your old family doctor. New knowledge and breakthroughs in medicine have eliminated the GP as we once knew him. He has now been replaced by a more highly educated variation known as the family physician. According to Marla J. Tobin, MD, family physicians now provide medical care in ninety-three percent of U.S. counties.

Most family physicians are able to provide comprehensive medical services to all family members regardless of age, beginning with newborns. A few provide obstetrical services as well, though most of these serve patients primarily in the rural areas where specialists are less common. A well-trained and experienced family physician can treat *ninety-five percent* of all problems afflicting children and adults. In addition, nearly all family physicians have special training in the areas of preventive health, sports medicine, geriatrics, and numerous office surgical procedures.

Family physicians are trained in all areas of women's health including adolescence, psychosocial issues, sexuality, contraception, pregnancy, menopause, and diseases of the reproductive tract. There are also new areas such as alternative therapies, osteoporosis, domestic violence and substance abuse that have caught the attention of family physicians according to Dr. Marla J.Tobin as published in an article, "The Family Physician of the 21st. Century", *The Female Patient*, January, 2000.

Some families beyond the childbearing age may choose to see a general internist as their PCP. Specialists in internal medicine usually do not see patients under the age of sixteen. As compared to family physicians, internists tend to perform fewer gynecological services and fewer office surgical procedures. General internists are more involved in hospital work and often treat an older population of patients. Many even specifically concentrate in caring for the geriatric population.

Some mothers prefer to have their children cared for by a pediatrician who can also function as a PCP for the younger family members. Occasionally, pediatricians will follow patients into early adulthood, but this varies with different physicians and patients. Pediatricians are best able to provide services for the unusually sick newborn and the more critically ill child.

Many women experiencing gynecological problems feel most comfortable with a specialist in the field of OB-GYN. The services provided by this specialty are limited to obstetrics, contraception, fertility, specific female diseases and some breast disease management. On the other hand, Dr. Tobin noted in the article, "The Family Physician of the 21st. Century," "At the dawning of the new millennium, it is the family physician, perhaps more than any other clinician, who is working with the female patient to synthesize the multitude of new diagnostic technologies and treatment modalities into a personal map for lifelong care." As one can see there are frequent difficult choices.

According to a recent article on the cost of medicine, by Kevin Fiscella, MD, and Peter Franks, MD, in *The Journal of Family Practice*, January, 2000, many studies show that family physicians generate lower patient costs than internists. They also charge less, order fewer laboratory tests, refer patients less frequently and generate less overall costs.

The family physician is a personal physician who practices comprehensive, scientific and humanistic medicine oriented around an individual in the context of the family. The **true artist** in family medicine looks for a challenge, explores problems in depth, and to the best of his ability attempts to help people live useful and meaningful lives.

There is no one specialty that is ideal for every patient and every situation. There are fortunately several choices we have to chose from. One must give careful consideration to the type of primary care physician that will best suit their needs and the needs of their family and then do the best they can to find the perfect one.

One point I believe that all primary care physicians should agree on was made by a family physician, Dr. Doug Iliff, from Topeka, Kansas in an article reported in *Family Practice Management*, January, 2000. **"As it has always been, the greatest challenge for family physicians will be to uphold the intergrity of the profession by doing what is best for our patients, putting ourselves second."**

Chapter 8

Selecting a Specific Physician

WE NEED TO CHOSE OUR PHYSICIANS WISELY

*"The great error of our day in the treatment of the
human body is that physicians separate the soul from
the body."*

--Socrates

If medical insurance issues are not a concern, then selecting a specific physician may be a simple process. One may simply seek care from a physician previously known to the family. Under the current medical climate, however, this scenario is the exception and not the rule – unless you live in rural areas not yet under the wing of managed care. Those who have recently moved to a new area are often faced with no knowledge of the local medical community unless this information is available through their place of work. Should one be employed and insured through their work, it is often necessary to visit a physician listed under the umbrella of their company's health insurance plan. Asking for a physician referral from a co-worker who is pleased with their physician may be helpful in shortening your search.

Another excellent source of information may be local churches or synagogues. Drop by and introduce yourself to your new priest, minister, rabbi, or other religious leader. Many of them will be familiar with physicians in the area, and they will often prove to be a reliable source.

Local pharmacists are terrific sources of information and are knowledgeable members of the health care team. It is surprising how much they know about local physicians, based on what they have heard from their clients and what they know about their prescribing habits. One day a new patient visited my office for the first time. When asked how she had been referred, she

41

commented, "I asked the pharmacist at the Revco down the street and he recommended you. He said your prescriptions are carefully written and you're very conscientious about returning phone calls when necessary." Introduce yourself to a pharmacist in your neighborhood and explain that you want to seek the expertise of a nearby physician. Your pharmacist may be happy to give you a referral, knowing you'll eventually be back for needed prescriptions.

It is interesting how people sometimes choose physicians when none is really known to them. When looking through directories, many choose physicians based on a convenient location. Many also select doctors based on the physician's name or nationality. Of course, it is important to select someone who is able to speak your language if it is other than English – although large university medical centers and institutions similar to The Cleveland Clinic Foundation are usually able to provide interpreters. Working with interpreters, however, is not always ideal, since much can be lost in the interpretation of a problem. Local medical societies may have lists of bilingual physicians, and when available these can be your best option. Many hospitals offer referral services to local residents, and community hospitals often maintain current lists of doctors who are accepting new patients. In this era of mass and frequent migration as well as changing insurance patterns, few medical practices are closed unless a physician is retiring and winding down his practice.

Arranging A Get-Acquainted Visit

Once you have chosen a particular physician, your job isn't over. It is wise to arrange for a get-acquainted visit to determine if you feel comfortable with your new choice. Is the chemistry right? Does the physician have the appropriate credentials? Is the physician a board-certified specialist? Does the physician have a caring personality? Does the doctor seem to be attentive and a good listener? Many of these questions can only be answered by a get-acquainted visit.

42

Listening to a patient's concerns is the most important quality of a good physician. One of the most frequent reasons patients give when changing physicians is that their physician failed to appear to listen to their problems. If a physician doesn't listen, he or she will come across as being rushed and uncaring. A physician who fails to listen carefully will also often overlook the primary reason why their patient scheduled their appointment in the first place. Physicians who listen carefully, however, discover the real essence of their patient's visit and convey to their patients a sense of empathy. Caring physicians will still be respected, even when results are borderline or lacking.

As you can see, selecting a new physician under emergency circumstances is not in one's best interest. Trying to find a doctor you like may require a preliminary visit to see if the chemistry between you and your physician is right.

Scheduling an initial get-acquainted visit also allows you the opportunity to see firsthand how your new doctor thinks and functions. It provides you with an opportunity to observe how his office functions. During your initial visit, you will have the opportunity to inquire about your new physician's professional interests, the ages of patients he or she feels most comfortable with, how urgent problems are handled, when you can expect phone calls to be returned, and how prescription refills are handled – to mention only a few issues.

Get-acquainted visits are often free of charge if no medical care is requested nor provided. Occasionally, there is a nominal fee, since some professional time is involved. When calling your new physician's office, explain that you wish to become a new patient and want to spend only a few moments with the doctor to see what he or she is like and to gain a better understanding of their philosophy. It also might be wise to explain to the office assistant that you do not intend to discuss a medical problem but simply want to say hello and meet with your new physician. This is not an unreasonable request and would most likely be granted at no charge – assuming the encounter is brief and unencumbered by medical concerns or requests. Visiting with at least two or three physicians would be a wise policy for any new patient, since careful selection is advisable when considering a long-term relationship.

" While many health care trends quickly come and go, health care in the new millennium may be shaped by these following characteristics. First, patients will be seeking care as 'educated consumers' more aware of both what they think they want and whom they want it from."

Marc L. Rivo, MD, MPH
Family Practice Management,
January 2000

Chapter 9

Doctor Hopping

Some patients, after seeing a physician several times, remain unsatisfied with the care they have received. That is certainly understandable, and in such cases shopping around for another physician may be prudent. Sometimes, however, patients have preconceived ideas about what they believe is wrong and how it should be handled. Even though their physician may see things differently, this does not sway them from seeking other opinions. Sooner or later, someone will find a physician who will agree with his or her point of view, right or wrong, since the practice of medicine remains an art form.

If you have seen two or more physicians who *do not* support your ideas, you may be misguided and need to re-evaluate your medical situation. I have known several patients who have flitted from one doctor to another, never fully satisfied with anyone's care. These insecure individuals have been unable to secure a trusting relationship with any physician. This can be the result of fear, unsuccessful past experiences, or related to other psychological issues such as anxiety or depression. Some patients do not wish to be dependent on physicians or medications and choose to look for other solutions.

On occasion, patients do suffer from unusual problems which can only be resolved by their perseverance. I remember one situation in the 1980s in which I had seen a middle-aged teacher on several occasions for chronic abdominal pain for which I could not find a reasonable explanation. The usual testing followed by several courses of medication failed to resolve her symptoms. She eventually grew tired of my attempts to help, and as a last resort, I decided to treat her for a depression she didn't have. Shortly thereafter she found a gastroenterologist who diagnosed an unusual intestinal parasitic disorder that when treated resolved her abdominal pain. Being quite upset over my missed diagnosis, she sent me a scathing letter describing my incompetence. Parasitic diseases are fairly uncommon to primary care physicians and can be easily overlooked. They occur in patients exposed to contaminated well water, ponds or small lakes. Parasitic infections can also occur in patients who work with livestock. Since I was a city slicker, I was not fully aware of these problems. Of course I learned a valuable lesson from this patient's unhappy experiences.

Her letter was one of those letters that has served my patients and me well over the years. Since that incident I have found several other cases of intestinal parasites that I would have probably overlooked had I not been appropriately educated by this unhappy patient. As you can see, letter writing can sometimes pay off, by helping other patients as well as physicians. If doctors accept unfavorable letters as educational tools rather than denunciations, they can reap positive benefits from them.

Generally, after thoroughly examining a patient, it is uncommon for a physician to miss important problems. Many patients suffering from confusing symptoms may in fact be suffering from an underlying anxiety or depressive disorder. This is especially true if you have seen several physicians without reaching a successful conclusion to your problem. Using psychological testing by a well-trained psychologist will often prove to be enlightening, since psychological counseling may help resolve problems that cannot be resolved by traditional medical methods.

In general, patients always feel better when their problems can be categorized into a specific disease, thereby allowing for a specific treatment. Although this may sound easy, it is not always possible. As research progresses, more difficult or unusual syndromes will be more easily diagnosed and properly managed.

Chapter 10

Moving to a New City

Many family physicians have a reference manual in their office listing family physicians practicing in other cities throughout America. The physicians found in these manuals will generally have qualifications similar to those of your own physician. Before moving, ask your physician for the name of a family doctor practicing in your new community. He or she will often be able to provide one. Also sign a release form allowing for transfer of medical records from your current doctor to your new family physician. Medical records are forwarded free of charge to other physicians.

Many patients forget to locate another physician after moving. Do not wait for a crisis to occur and then hope to find a physician that will see you. A well-established physician may be unable to provide an appointment at the last minute, even though you have an urgent medical problem. Take the initiative to find a qualified physician in your new hometown while you are healthy and feeling fine. This will avoid the inevitable delays that can accompany a serious situation if you have not already established a relationship with a physician. As you remember in the first chapter; Linda made many of these same avoidable errors.

Chapter 11

Physician Extenders and How They Help

In this era of belt tightening, one way physicians preserve capital is to hire additional staff, or physician extenders, to help them manage their practice. In some cases a well-trained and experienced nurse can perform a few limited duties by obtaining historical facts, taking test specimens, and administering injections. The pressures of managed care have encouraged the use of physician extenders, otherwise known as nurse practitioners or physician assistants, depending on their background and education. These professionals are most commonly found in large offices or group practices.

Catherine Holzheimer, R.N., a nurse practitioner student, describes the nurse practitioner as a registered nurse with both an advanced education (a master's degree or Ph.D.) and the clinical competency necessary for the delivery of primary health and medical care. They are licensed by state boards as advanced practice nurses after taking a national certification exam. Due to their expanded knowledge base when compared to nurses, nurse practitioners are able to initiate care plans, diagnose common illnesses, perform physical examinations, and in many states prescribe medications. They work in an outpatient setting – in collaboration with physicians – to assess, diagnose, develop and implement treatment plans for patients. Like family physicians, they have a special interest in promoting wellness and preventive health care. Nurse practitioners see patients during routine visits, for acute non-life threatening illnesses, and also for follow-up visits after chronic conditions such as hypertension or diabetes have been diagnosed. Nurse practitioners may function independent of a physician, but only in a limited fashion.

Another kind of physician extender is the physician assistant (PA). Over thirty years ago, a group of physicians perceived that they could deliver health care more effectively if they worked with assistants who were trained in medicine and could practice under physician supervision. Known as PAs, these assistants are now used in all medical and surgical specialties. Because PAs are trained under curriculums and faculties similar to those of physicians, they develop a form of medical reasoning that is similar to physicians'. In many primary care practices, PAs handle common patient problems, follow-up visits, and patient education. When they need advice or more advanced knowledge, they turn to their supervising physician for help.

Physician assistants' backgrounds are somewhat different from nurse practitioners, but their roles are quite similar. Some physician assistants have also served as medics in the armed forces, often side-by-side with physicians. With expanded training and experience, they can provide many of the services of physicians, although they must always function under a supervising physician. According to John Booher, a physician assistant at The Cleveland Clinic Foundation, physician assistants are licensed directly under their collaborating physician's medical license. PAs may practice in a location other than their physician's, but they consult with their physician whenever the need arises.

There are some differences between nurse practitioners and PAs. Nurse practitioners may think more independently, for instance, and focus more on patient education than PAs. PAs are more likely to perform technical duties such as applying casts, splints, or braces, and they also assist physicians as surgical assistants and in the management of postoperative care.

Generally, patients appreciate the care given by both nurse practitioners and physician assistants. This is due partly to the fact that these physician extenders have more time to devote to individual patients; they are not as hurried as many physicians. Frequently they will spend thirty minutes with a patient in a single visit. The additional time allows them the opportunity to provide more educational information than physicians might.

Overall, physician extenders are assets to the medical community. There are some potential problems with physician extenders, however, that patients must understand. Some physician extenders have the tendency to believe their knowledge base is equal to or even greater than that of the physician. Although in some cases this may in a limited sense

50

be true, they nonetheless lack the in-depth education and broad experience of physicians. They are less capable than physicians, for instance, of understanding a new illness or problem, and they therefore may be more likely to misdiagnose the problem. This can be a problem, since the key to good medical care is for the caregiver to understand an illness and arrive at an accurate diagnosis. Once a diagnosis is firmly established the options available for treatment become more obvious, though the management of a medical problem is sometimes not as simple as a physician extender may want to believe. If after seeing a physician extender you feel a more in-depth analysis of your problem is warranted, you may ask that a physician evaluate your case.

Currently, physician extenders are more commonplace in large centers or in rural areas where physicians are lacking. If you are satisfied with the care provided by physician extenders, your routine health maintenance visits to these professionals can supplement the care provided by physicians – often at reduced cost.

Chapter 12

Specialists

Most medical problems are initially best handled by your primary care physician. He is trained to provide medical care for ninety-five percent of all problems that confront the average patient. On occasion your family physician or internist will recognize that your situation may require the expertise of a specialist. Surgical problems, cancer, abnormal cardiac rhythms, and complex medical diseases may require you to see one or more specialists. Your family physician is familiar with the health care system and is best suited to refer you when the need arises. This is not only true for complex diseases but is especially true under urgent or emergency circumstances.

I can provide two examples of how, under difficult circumstances, I was able to provide emergency assistance for patients who were seen at my office at one time or another. While working in a family practice center at Fairview General Hospital in Cleveland, Ohio, a mother came to my office with a two-year-old child who had been complaining of a severe sore throat. He was drooling and unable to swallow his own secretions. From this presentation, I suspected a life-threatening disorder known as acute epiglottitis. The epiglottis is a small structure above the larynx or voice box that when inflamed from a bacterial infection can swell enough to block one's airway. Should this occur, suffocation can rapidly lead to death. Without looking into the child's throat – a maneuver that could have caused immediate death from gagging or choking – I picked up the child and began running towards the operating room instructing my nurse to alert surgery that I was on the way. Moving as fast as possible, I ran with the child to the nearest available surgical suite, where an anesthesiologist was waiting for me. The child was immediately intubated (a tube passed into the trachea) to prevent suffocation. After having his airway protected, the child was admitted to ICU for intravenous antibiotic therapy. He was later released after a rapid and successful recovery from a life threatening illness.

On another occasion, during my first year of practice in the 1970s, a mother came to my office in Columbia, South Carolina with her young child. She claimed he had been bitten on his foot by a black widow spider. The spider had been residing in the child's shoe. I wondered how she could be so certain that the spider was a black widow. She presented a jar containing the dead spider. Sure enough, it was a large black spider with the characteristic hourglass markings on its abdomen. I said, "Follow me to the emergency room," and off we went. For some reason, on that particular day no emergency room physician was in attendance. I asked the head emergency room nurse, "Who's the local expert on the management of black widow bites?" She paused for a second and then while looking me straight in the eye she said, "You are. We haven't seen one of these in ten years."

The situation was anxiety-provoking; particularly, since I had never seen a black widow bite before. I decided to start an intravenous line and to prepare for the worst. Fortunately, the child was medically stable, at least for the moment. It occurred to me however, that this child's best chance would be provided by the use of an anti-venom. I conducted a preliminary skin test on the child's arm to check for evidence of a possible allergic reaction to the black widow anti-venom. The boy developed a mild redness at the injection sight from the test dose of anti-venom. Fortunately, he did not break out with hives, nor did he develop breathing difficulties – two indications that he might be allergic to the anti-venom. Feeling secure enough that the child was not allergic to the black widow anti-venom, I decided to administer the full dose. He was then admitted to the ICU for further treatment and observation. The young boy experienced an uneventful recovery and was released in good health a few days later.

Under most circumstances, before seeing a specialist, it is best to contact your primary care physician for initial care or advice. They are capable of delivering excellent care and most often no referrals will be necessary. Should you require a referral, your primary care physician is best equipped to arrange for it. He will take into account your own situation as well as several other factors before referring you to a specific specialist. Many patients, and rightly so, are concerned about a physician's bedside manner. Others believe a physician's knowledge and technical abilities are most important. To obtain the best fit, it is best to review your thoughts and concerns with your doctor before the time of a referral. Too often, patients keep their ideas to themselves, and then are dissatisfied with the specialist to whom they were referred. Many physicians are excellent technicians providing the best in surgical expertise. Some fall short since specialists will sometimes lack a pleasant bedside manner. In the field of medicine, many patients incorrectly equate a physician's bedside manner with his level of medical expertise. Fortunately for many physicians, patients vary on the level of social graces they demand of their physicians.

As a patient, try to become aware of your needs and seek a physician that fulfills them. When your doctor has a complete understanding of your medical, emotional and social needs he will then be able to provide the proper help, referring you appropriately to the best medical facility or specialist when the time comes. Some specialists have special skills or unique experiences, and others are familiar with a special technique. Your family physician may be the best informed and best able to refer you to a specialist that will most adequately serve your needs. Simply selecting a specialist from a list in a phone directory or insurance manual may not be in your best interest.

After a consultant has seen you, it is usually wise to return to your family doctor to review what transpired and to plan future care. Specialists, after providing appropriate care, generally forward a letter to your primary care physician describing what was found, his diagnosis, the treatment plan and future follow-up care that may be needed. Usually, after reviewing this information, your family physician will fully agree with the specialist's recommendations and follow through with them. Only on rare occasions will your family doctor disagree with a specialist. When it happens, your primary care physician sometimes requests a second opinion.

Generally, unless your status suddenly changes, it will not be necessary for you to return regularly to the specialist. Contemporary family doctors are more highly trained than the general practitioners of old, and they are comfortable in providing routine follow-up care for many conditions that in the past were managed only by specialists. Annual or semiannual visits to the specialist, however, may still be warranted to determine if any fine-tuning is necessary.

If you are sensitive about personalities, gender, or other character traits, it may be best to mention your concerns to your doctor before you have been referred. Sometimes your primary care physician will know the specialist quite well as a friend and as a professional. Your doctor may then be able to provide a synopsis of what he or she is like. In this era of managed care, however, the "old connections" may no longer be available as they once were. In the past, doctors had traveled in relatively comfortable circles, referring to only two or three surgeons, two or three gynecologists, and so forth. They grew to know their small circle of specialists and were able to adjust to their practice patterns, to various idiosyncrasies and to patient requests. These relationships had many advantages, some of the most important being the ability to offer quick and reliable referrals for their patients with a simple phone call. Now it is not uncommon, especially in large metropolitan areas, for doctors to have no familiarity at all with most of the physicians listed in your insurance directory. This lack of familiarity may result in less personalized service.

Once a specialist has been selected, you will usually see that specialist as soon as possible. Your specialist will perform a lengthy, detailed evaluation of your problem. Since he or she is an expert in a limited field, the specialist will be specific and deliberate when looking for key symptoms. Often the specialist will order key tests, specialized procedures or biopsies of suspicious areas when necessary. Sometimes new medications or treatments will be started. Your specialists may want to see you two or even three times to review tests and to determine if you are responding to their therapy. Sometimes the specialist will need to order additional studies should your problem persist.

Once stable and doing well, patients will then be asked to return to their primary care physician for ongoing medical care. The specialist will forward to your primary care physician a comprehensive letter describing his findings and recommendations.

The specialist may recommend a change in medications prescribed by your PCP. The specialist often requests that your family physician or general internist refer you back for a periodic follow up visit. This is more likely to occur when you are suffering from chronic illnesses.

Frequently communication delays occur between specialists and referring physicians. With that in mind, it is wise to take careful note of what your specialist discussed during your most recent visit. Be prepared to list any medications that had been prescribed or recommendations offered. These facts will come in handy when visiting your family doctor, particularly if he has not received the specialist's letter before your visit. Do the best you can to work with the system and keep track of what has transpired. Being well prepared will improve your satisfaction level as well as the ultimate outcome. Should you feel dissatisfied or mystified after seeing a specialist, you may request that your PCP arrange for a second opinion. After you have received a second opinion, return to your family doctor to review the different opinions of the specialists.

Your family doctor can generally answer any remaining questions and assist you in your deliberations. Many family physicians are very people-oriented and can clear up misconceptions or misunderstandings should the need arise. Should you still remain perplexed, your PCP can call consultants on your behalf to help sort out troubling issues. Do not be timid when it comes to looking for help with important health care problems. More often than not, you will be pleasantly surprised by your PCP's willingness to help in difficult situations. Most physicians hope to please their patients by helping them remain comfortable with their ongoing care.

Overuse of specialists who perform expensive procedures or diagnostic studies has led to strict control and management of these services by primary care physicians. When specialists

57

must be seen, your doctor will select from those listed in your insurance manual. Always try to remember to bring your health insurance manual with you when visiting your primary care physician. It will often come in handy.

Most plans require substantial copays by patients who insist on frequenting specialists not enrolled in their plan. The majority of plans provide for competent physicians in all areas of medical expertise; although, a frequent complaint of patients in urban areas is that their offices may not be conveniently located. On rare occasions, a specific physician not listed on your plan may have a unique area of expertise that you require. Should this occur, it is not unreasonable to request a referral beyond the normal scope of your plan.

A few patients believe that they can see anyone they wish if their PCP approves the referral. This is often not true; although, occasionally your physician will attempt to go beyond the limits of your plan. However, the abuse of this tactic by a physician may lead to ultimate termination of your doctor as a preferred provider in your health plan. Since it is difficult for primary care physicians to be accepted as providers on some plans, they do not give carefree referrals – preferring to follow the guidelines established by health care contracts.

Lately, patients – as well as government officials – have been losing patience with excessively strict insurance guidelines, and some degree of relief may be forthcoming in legislation that may be enacted in the not-too-distant future. It is refreshing to note that one health care insurance company, United Healthcare, with headquarters in Minnetonka, Minnesota, has independently decided to improve patient and physician satisfaction through a new policy announced November 9, 1999, referred to as Care Coordination. This limited program gives some control back to "excellent physicians who make good decisions with patients". In days gone by, physicians made all decisions related to patient care and management. Over the past ten years insurance companies have usurped much of these responsibilities to control costs that health care plans felt were excessive. Newer thinking is now swinging back again towards more control by physicians who practice good quality care while still controlling costs. This scenario may prove to be the best of both worlds. Time will allow us to see which arrangements will provide the highest degree of patient satisfaction.

Chapter 13

Physical Therapists

Many medical conditions, as well as acute injuries, can be treated with the application of physical therapy. A referral for physical therapy is an opportunity to gain knowledge as well as help for your condition. A therapist will teach you about the biomechanics of your joints and muscles and show you how various exercises may help your recovery. The physical therapist will also provide insight about factors that may have contributed to your problem and information about how to modify these factors to avoid future re-injury. Re-injury can often be avoided by altering how things are done at home or at work to reduce risk, pain, and disability. Receiving care from physical therapists can relieve and improve many muscle or skeletal problems resulting in a faster and more complete recovery. Most importantly, if you adhere to your therapy, you can expect improved strength, dexterity and range of motion of injured parts. All too often many patients fail to follow through with their physical therapist's recovery plan.

Physical therapists are trained in applying the principles of exercise, hot and cold applications, massage, ultrasound and other modalities to aid in your return to normal health. The ultimate goal of physical therapy is to achieve normal or close-to-normal function and to relieve or eliminate pain. After attending several sessions, you may acquire enough skills and knowledge to carry on independently at home while trying to improve your condition. An exercise prescription will be given to you to follow on a daily basis.

Upon entering a physical therapy facility you will notice numerous pieces of equipment. Each piece of equipment is designed to achieve a specific goal. Some pieces of exercise equipment are used to assist in your return to normal health. Others, such as upper and lower extremity bikes, may be used for warm-up activities. Later, other pieces of equipment may improve the function of a specific body part such as your

61

shoulders, hips, or knees. Strengthening equipment such as leg presses and shoulder pulley systems may be used as well. Large therapeutic rubber balls provide for a variety of activities to help patients recover from low back strain and to assist others in regaining muscle coordination prior to their return to sports. Used correctly, most equipment will also improve your endurance.

In addition to equipment at the facility, patients may be given equipment for home use. Many neck related injuries, for example, can be relieved through the use of cervical traction equipment attached to a bedroom door. Stretching exercises are helpful in reducing muscle spasm in the injured neck while relieving pain and promoting healing at the same time.

Patients are often asked to perform repetitive exercises at home through the use of large therapeutic rubber bands that may be attached to furniture legs, doorknobs or other fixed structures. By providing resistance to weakened muscle groups, such exercises will improve strength, muscle tone, and shape. When necessary, patients may be asked to purchase hand or ankle weights from sporting goods stores to aid in their recovery.

Physical therapy modalities such as on-sight ultrasound and electrical stimulation equipment are also available for use by a skilled physical therapist to reduce pain and muscle spasm. Your physician will order some of these modalities while others are used when needed on the advice of experienced therapists. Facilities without adequate and up to date equipment should be passed over in favor of more modern options.

Physical therapy is not for everyone. Some patients have returned to my office complaining that the exercises or treatments have worsened their problem. If this turns out to be the case, discuss your lack of progress with your therapist. Later, if necessary, discuss the problem with your physician. Sometimes there are simple reasons why you may not be improving, and your therapist can change your program as needed to adjust to your particular needs.

Several common pitfalls may contribute to lack of progress. Performing exercises incorrectly is one of these. Tammy Murray, a physical therapist with The Cleveland Clinic

Foundation, commented, "Remember, physical therapy is a *prescription* for exercise and as such needs to be followed as prescribed by your therapist and doctor if it is to work properly for the condition being treated." Some patients may be exercising too much or too often, believing if they do well with ten repetitions they'll improve even more rapidly with thirty or forty repetitions. Usually, however, this is not the case. Sticking with your therapist's recommendations is the wisest course of action.

Similarly, there are those that do not perform enough of the required exercises. Some patients have good intentions, but fail to complete recommended programs due to scheduling or work-related problems. Others fail to use the proper exercise form as demonstrated by their therapist, resulting in potential failure or even worsening of their symptoms. Some patients have a tendency to compare their problems with those of their friends or relatives who may have had similar difficulties. This is a mistake, since everyone's injury is unique.

As you can see, many factors may contribute to your recovery. Your recovery will vary with the extent of your injury, lifestyle and occupation. Patients are often reluctant to question treatment programs, thinking this is the way the system works and this is what can be expected. Be open and honest in communication with your therapist. As members of your health care team, you and your therapist are in it together.

SECTION III: THE OFFICE VISIT

Chapter 14

Appointment Scheduling: How It Works & How to Make It Work

Before you go through the process of scheduling an appointment at your primary care physician's office, it would be helpful for you to have a clear understanding of how most medical offices run. Of course, the secret of any effective organization is to have good leadership and a knowledgeable and caring staff.

The most important aspect of an efficient medical office boils down to good communication and accurate scheduling of medical visits. Family physician David C. Kibbe, MD, MBA, and chief executive officer of Future Health Care, Inc., commented in *Family Practice Magazine*, January 2000, "We must manage our practices in a manner that satisfies our customer's needs for information, access and convenience because the consumer will be the driver in the health care marketplace." Good communication must begin with effective handling of phone calls, an area of medical care given top priority by patients, an issue that will be handled in greater detail in the next chapter.

Scheduling Appointments

It is important to note here, that one should always request adequate help from your physician's office staff in order to schedule your office visit appropriately. Accurately discussing your needs with an appointment secretary will usually result in satisfactory scheduling and adequate time required to assess your problems.

Regardless of the professional abilities of your physician, you will not be satisfied when dealing with his office unless routine business practices are taken care of first. The process of scheduling appointments is not rocket science, but many doctor's offices make it seem that it is. All too often, patients suffer unreasonable waits – with the excuse of an *unexpected emergency*. In fact, however, real emergencies are generally the exception, not the rule.

The process of scheduling appointments begins with determining how much time must be allotted to each patient's problem. Each physician generally has in mind an approximate amount of time that is required to provide a specific service. Your physician will often determine a specific amount of time that he will need each day for dealing with activities such as physical examinations, routine office visits, urgent office visits, surgical procedures, PAP tests and other physical examinations.

Well-organized physicians can estimate this time fairly accurately. Usually, each hour of office time is broken down into ten to fifteen minute intervals. Most office visits, for example, are scheduled for a single ten- or fifteen-minute time slot. One or more time slots can be assigned to each patient. The length of the visit or the number of time slots scheduled per patient varies with the needs of the patient. A new patient visit may be scheduled for thirty minutes, since the physician will be unfamiliar with the patient and his or her needs. Sometimes with a completely healthy patient a first visit or get-acquainted visit may be brief, lasting only a few minutes. This situation is especially true if no medical services were required. Some physicians, however, always require thirty to sixty minutes during an initial visit to fully assess a patient, regardless of that patient's health status. The amount of time spent per patient visit varies with a physician's philosophy. Comprehensive physical exams are very time-consuming, and in primary care settings they are often reserved for only one or two appointment slots per day.

Longer-than-average appointment times may be set aside for surgical procedures, PAP tests or specialized exams such as sigmoidoscopies. Which procedures a doctor performs in his or her office will vary from practice to practice.

Many primary care physicians include several open time slots per day in their schedule to handle the urgent problems that will inevitably occur. It has always been my policy to have approximately four urgent time slots set aside each morning during routine office hours. I have also followed the same policy by assigning an additional four urgent slots for afternoon or evening use to treat problems that should not wait until the next day. Should you find it difficult to see your physician for acute problems, **you may suggest** that he or she add additional urgent appointment slots to their daily schedule by reducing the number of routine appointment slots they would usually have.

After a schedule has been established, the goal of each physician is to keep the office visits within the time frame that has been allotted. Your physician can rapidly fall behind schedule if these time slots are not respected. If, for example, thirty patients have been scheduled to be seen in an eight-hour workday, and your physician runs over each visit by a single minute, by noon he will be fifteen minutes behind schedule. Therefore, patients seen in the early afternoon will have to wait a minimum of fifteen minutes as a direct result of the morning back-up.

It is sometimes difficult to keep on time without giving a patient the feeling of being rushed. How well a physician can accomplish this task varies with experience, the stresses of the day, emergency phone calls, and so forth.

In summary, both patients and physicians play a major role in how well a medical office functions. When scheduling an office visit, try to be aware both of your needs and those of the physician. Try to stay within the original framework planned for your visit. In other words, if you were scheduled to discuss problems A and B, it would not be fair to unexpectedly request further help on problems C and D – which you did not mention when scheduling your appointment. If a new and more serious problem has occurred since scheduling your appointment, it may be wise to inform your doctor of this from the start of your office visit. He or she will then be able to select and treat the problems that are the most urgent, and then ask you to reschedule another office visit to cover the others. Attempting to cover too much ground in a single appointment will often result in less-than-adequate attention to any one of your problems.

On Time Appointment Scheduling:

A subset of appointment scheduling is arranging for appointments in a timely fashion. Many patients wait until the last minute to arrange for visits they know they have to schedule. Some become upset when their needs cannot be comfortably met. Several examples reflect this scenario. On a daily basis patients call for appointments because they are about to run out of needed medications that require follow-up evaluation. They hoped to be squeezed in but accommodating last minute nonurgent matters can be taxing to a busy office. On par with this is the need for last minute appointments required by children for school entrance physicals, camp physicals or sports physicals. Towards the end of the summer there is always a bunch of freshmen college students requiring admission physicals calling a few days before they leave for school. Because most universities require physical exams, it is prudent to schedule an office visit during the summer even if your college physical forms have not arrived. Students must also remember to bring in previous immunization records from other physicians when indicated. Universities require proof of immunizations before admission. If immunization records are not available blood testing to verify immunity will have to be conducted or new injections administered. Neither of these alternatives are met with enthusiasm. Always look at home for old records of childhood immunizations when proof of immunity is required. When all else fails, immunization records may be available from your child's board of education. Just as importantly you should schedule office visits with ample time to correct for deficiencies.

Chapter 15

Phoning and Visiting Your Primary Care Physician's Office

Entering the health care system generally begins with a phone call to your primary care physician. A little extra planning before the phone call will be helpful in the long run. Before you make your phone call, it is important to write down answers to a few of the questions that the appointment secretary will ask you. If the secretary does not in fact ask you for some of this information, be prepared to offer it to reduce the chance of mis-scheduling your appointment.

No medical office is perfect. Some have a fairly high turnover of office personnel. Some assistants have not been fully trained. Some are inexperienced. Some may be harried or simply moody. The role of the appointment secretary is difficult at best, considering the demands placed upon her by both patients and caregivers. Patients may have to pick up the slack and assist whenever possible in providing essential information, so that their appointment is properly scheduled.

After your phone call has been received, provide your full name and – if the patient is someone other than you – the name and age of that patient. If the patient is insured, provide the name of the medical insurance company, especially if the patient is a member of a managed care health plan or HMO. Insured patients are usually limited to care provided by a specific list of primary care physician panel members listed in their medical insurance handbooks. An appointment secretary is generally familiar with the health plans that their physicians serve. In the case of large medical groups, keeping current on the activity of all contracts negotiated by the group's business office may be difficult for some appointment secretaries. In these cases, it is the responsibility of patients to be aware of which physicians are primary care providers under their health plan. After establishing that the physician you have chosen is a provider, then you may proceed.

Sometimes the manner in which you were initially referred to your new physician is a point worth clarifying when making your first appointment. Were you a self-referral? Were you referred by another patient, hospital or specialist? This information is helpful for the office staff to know, in case your records will need to be acquired or your information forwarded to a referring physician.

When scheduling your appointment, you should explain to the medical secretary the specific goals you wish to achieve during your visit with the doctor. Do you wish to simply become acquainted with your new physician? Do you wish to schedule a physical exam? Do you have a list of problems you need to have evaluated? Be as specific as possible. The more clearly the appointment secretary understands your needs the more likely adequate time will be provided for your upcoming visit. Scheduling appointments is an art form best accomplished when each party fully communicates with the other.

Your initial office visit may serve several useful purposes. One of the most important things it does is to commit your new physician to providing ongoing medical care for you. Until you have actually been seen by your physician, simply selecting him as an intended physician for future care has no binding aspects, nor does it require him to assist you under urgent circumstances. At any given point in time, hundreds of prospective patients could notify their health plan that they have decided to select a specific physician, but until they have actually been seen as a patient, their intentions represent only an idea – and not a commitment by anyone.

If only one individual in a family has been seen by their primary care physician, it doesn't necessarily imply that all other family members have the same status. Usually after one family member has been seen, your physician may also consider other family members as patients, but this will vary from practice to practice. Certainly, any other family member with ongoing medical problems should likewise arrange to be seen under routine circumstances. One should not wait for a crisis to occur and then find out that scheduling for an urgent visit is difficult at best. Established patients always have priority over potential patients when it comes to the provision of urgent care.

Once your initial or get-acquainted visit has been completed you are then established as a full-fledged member of your doctor's practice. Physicians are bound ethically, medically, and legally to provide care to established patients and are therefore much more attentive to their needs. A physician that has never seen you as a patient has no obligation to "squeeze" you in regardless of how urgent your problems may be. That is not to say that physicians don't wish to accommodate those in need. It is simply the case that on a daily basis most physicians have many current patients in dire straits who must be attended to first. Therefore, you must establish yourself and other family members as patients early on before any services can be expected.

As mentioned earlier, office visits may take many forms. Likewise, patients usually have a specific agenda in mind when they call for an appointment. With proper planning, matching your needs to those of your physician's office is simple. It is worth mentioning once again the importance of listing your medical problems, if you have more than one, so that your appointment can be scheduled with adequate time to address each one of them.

Using Proper Terminology When Scheduling Your Appointment

Reviewing commonly used terminology before one calls for an appointment may be helpful in preventing the confusion that often runs rampant. Patients often use terms or phrases incorrectly, resulting in scheduling errors.

Many patients call in requesting to be seen for a "check-up." This unfortunate term has different meanings to everyone. To some, a check-up simply means having their cholesterol checked. To others, it may imply a review of their current medications. To a woman, it may be a request for their annual PAP and breast exam. To others, it may suggest a comprehensive head-to-toe evaluation. What a physician may consider a check-up and what a patient has in mind are often two entirely different things. One should be as specific as possible when requesting a check-up. Ask yourself what you want to have accomplished by your office visit? Some patients believe a check-up is a brief assessment of their overall health, and for healthy patients this may be the case. If a patient is relatively young, feels well, and has no complaints, a medical evaluation can be handled quickly and with little fanfare. However when a patient's condition deviates from that standard, the amount of time and effort required to perform an adequate evaluation can be considerable.

Adults with chronic illnesses or who use prescription medications on a daily basis should consider scheduling a complete or comprehensive physical evaluation for their first office visit. Even healthy younger adults should consider this form of evaluation every two years or so. Most physicians view a complete physical exam as an in-depth evaluation that provides a working baseline. For the sake of clarification, the terms complete or comprehensive are used interchangeably in the field of health care when associated with the term physical exam. A complete physical exam provides the setting to review previous problems as well as current symptoms and concerns. Once completed, it will serve as a satisfactory yardstick for future medical care. A complete physical evaluation will take between thirty to sixty minutes, not including additional time required for tests or x-rays that may be necessary. Due to the considerable time required for this type of evaluation, physicians rarely have set aside more than one or two appointment slots per day to perform complete physical exams. In some practices one should not be surprised to wait several weeks or months for an appointment of this type. You should thus plan accordingly should you require a thorough "check up" of this type.

One other word of caution: not all insurance companies will cover routine or complete physical exams. Even though these evaluations are often crucial to good preventive health care, insurance companies may view them differently. Insurance companies that cover the cost of complete physical exams will do so at specific intervals of time.

Appointment Length

As mentioned earlier, routine appointment times that vary in length from ten to fifteen minutes will usually accommodate most medical problems. During this time frame, one or two separate problems can be addressed, though follow-up visits are often necessary to access results, good, bad, or otherwise.

Sometimes a single complicated medical problem can take fifteen to thirty minutes by itself. Let's consider one of these possibilities. Evaluating a potentially complex problem such as chronic cough will initially take a fifteen-minute appointment. Causes of a persistent cough can vary from the very benign to some of the most serious of problems that patients must confront. Patients are often unaware of the complexity of many disorders thereby underestimating what must be done to adequately diagnose and treat them. On the surface, many problems appear to be simple but often are not. Competent physicians, while evaluating a patient, review a long list of possible causes that could be linked to their patient's problem. The list of possible causes for each problem being evaluated is referred to as a *differential diagnosis*. A differential diagnosis for every symptom is considered by your doctor during your office visit. Your doctor will then select the diagnosis that most closely matches your group of symptoms.

As mentioned above, chronic cough can have many different causes. A short list of possibilities would include infectious diseases of all varieties, asthma, hay fever, allergic rhinitis, throat and laryngeal tumors, cancers, chronic lung diseases and so on. As one can see, one must approach each medical problem with caution and patience. Time and testing is often required to sort out the causes of many symptoms.

To complicate matters further, patients will sometimes bring up late in an office visit a new and even more serious problem, hoping to have it resolved before they leave. For example, after a patient has had their cough evaluated, they may exclaim at the end of their visit, "Oh, by the way, lately I have been having terrible back pains." This is the type of situation that creates havoc in the practice of medicine. A fair amount of additional time would be required to satisfactorily address the problem of back pain. Certainly severe back pain is often a crippling problem that requires early attention. Should an additional problem such as back pain or unexplained chest pain suddenly surface after you have already called and arranged for your appointment, further action is necessary. Calling to alert the appointment secretary before your visit of additional concerns is usually a good idea. This will allow your physician's staff to alter the time frame of your appointment to better accommodate your needs.

Patients who believe they have complicated problems or several unrelated problems should request additional time when scheduling their appointment. Should you confront the appointment secretary with several problems needing to be evaluated, she may indicate that your doctor's time is limited for that particular day. If this occurs, then select the most pressing problem that you face and arrange for another appointment shortly thereafter to cover your other concerns. When beginning your office visit, briefly list for the doctor your problems – allowing both you and him to sort out which problems require immediate attention versus those that can wait. Occasionally, none of your problems can wait, and they all must be addressed at your current visit – though this situation tends to be the exception and not the rule. Your doctor will generally do the best he can to address all of your problems as quickly as possible.

How does one decide what is a complicated problem? Certainly, if you have been seen in the past by other physicians for the same problem, and it has gone unresolved, then additional time should be requested when scheduling your visit. If your problem has been difficult in the past to manage, it probably will remain so. Scheduling extra time for your office visit may be a good idea should your problems be multiple in nature or chronic in duration. Some patients with multiple problems may also be using several prescription drugs and therefore may require a double appointment slot to comfortably meet their needs. Please take your own personal circumstances into account when requesting an appointment so that your needs can be addressed thoroughly and in a satisfactory manner.

Research indicates a high percentage of patients have three separate problems per office visit they wish to have to have reviewed by their PCP. Specialists such as cardiologists or neurologists often schedule patients for fifteen to thirty minutes to evaluate and manage a single problem within the scope of their specialty. Primary care physicians are often expected by patients to evaluate or treat too many problems in a single visit. Many patients clearly underestimate the complexity of their symptoms often believing incorrectly that there is a quick or simple answer to every illness.

The PAP Test

Another common appointment that can be misunderstood or mis-scheduled is the annual female pelvic exam, or PAP test. Until recently, the PAP test invented by Dr. George Papanicolaou in the late 1940s, has been the best screening test to detect cervical cancer in its earliest stages – when it is easily curable. The PAP test is performed by passing a collection brush and a wooden spatula into the vagina where they are inserted into the cervical canal of the uterus to collect cells for diagnostic purposes. These cells are placed on a glass slide and then forwarded to a lab for analysis. It is of interest to note, that a new test to be reviewed later, has replaced the PAP test as the best method to diagnose cancer of the cervix. Though anxiety provoking for women because of the intimate nature of the pelvic exam, it is well tolerated by most.

A thorough breast exam, mini-physical exam and rectal exam are often included with the annual PAP test. If a woman has had a hysterectomy, most women believe – and correctly so – that a PAP test is not necessary. However, an annual breast exam, pelvic exam and rectal exam are still warranted to evaluate for various forms of cancer other than uterine or cervical cancer.

Many women will require mammography as well, and these tests should be scheduled at intervals delineated in the appendix.

When calling your physician's office to schedule your annual female exam, using the commonly recognized term "PAP test" rather than the less descriptive term "check-up" will reduce some scheduling errors. Try to schedule your appointment so that it's at least one week after your menstrual period. Avoid douching several days before your exam. Avoid contraceptive or lubricating jelly two to three days preceding your exam, and avoid intercourse one to two days beforehand. Taking these steps will increase the chances of obtaining an accurate test.

Other Check-ups

Visit your primary care physician for routine evaluations. A whole host of medical examinations serving a variety of useful purposes are frequently required throughout life . Some patients need work physicals while others need sports physicals. Many patients may require a life insurance exam to add or extend their insurance coverage. Middle-aged and older adults need a comprehensive physical exam along with exercise stress testing to determine whether or not they can safely participate in various activities at local health clubs. College physicals can be simple or complex. High school physicals can vary widely in requirements from one school system to another.

As one can see, the time and needs for physical exams may vary dramatically, depending on many circumstances. It's best when calling for an appointment to be as specific as possible about the purpose of your physical exam. When possible, call several weeks in advance to schedule your visit and fax or mail a copy of the required physical exam form, if any, to your physician's office. Your physician, after checking the form, will know how much time will be needed for your examination and what tests, if any, will be necessary. This process will result in accurate scheduling, satisfied patients and completion of important physical exams in a timely fashion and with the least amount of inconvenience for all involved.

Appointment Review

Finally, after you have carefully discussed your physical exam needs or your medical problem with the appointment secretary, one should review all of the pertinent information. Review the time and date of your upcoming office visit. A frequent problem with scheduling is the miscommunication of appointment details, either on the part of the secretary or on the part of the patient. We all make mistakes, so a little additional care will avoid unfortunate mishaps when the time comes. It's also helpful to note on your calendar with whom you spoke when scheduling your appointment. Should mis-scheduling occur, and if you are able to identify the party with whom you spoke, he/she will generally be much more accommodating to your needs.

The next point may seem silly, but if you are uncertain of your physician's office location, please clarify this point with his secretary. Over the course of their careers, physicians may practice out of more than one office location and even move their offices from time to time – unbeknownst to some of their patients. Their office phone number may remain the same, even though their office location has changed. On several occasions, some of my patients have gone to a previous medical office where I no longer practice. No matter how thorough one's office staff tries to be in notifying patients after a change of address, some patients will fall through the cracks. Computerized patient address lists may be inaccurate, incomplete, lost in the mail, or misplaced. It is important to verify the correct location before the day of your appointment, since going to the wrong address may result in your missing the appointment.

Appointment Cancellation

If you find that you will be unable to make it to your appointment, cancel it as far in advance as possible. Many patients fail to cancel their appointments, simply failing to show up as promised. At the time of scheduling an appointment, you have formally agreed to see your physician. Just as importantly, you have eliminated an opportunity for another patient – possibly one sicker than yourself – to see your physician. Should your needs or personal situation change and you wish to cancel your visit, please do so by calling your physician's office as soon as possible. Even with only one or two hours notice of a cancellation, other patients can be contacted to come in earlier than planned, thus opening up new appointment slots for the needy as the day progresses.

On the surface, appointment scheduling appears to be an innocuous event, but in fact it takes a lot of work. Good planning, preparation and follow-through should eliminate most recurrent scheduling problems. You as a patient can do much to ensure the smooth operation of the health care system. Conscientiousness on your part will serve you and others well.

Chapter 16

Preparing for Your Office Visit

Adequate preparation for most medical office visits requires some advance planning. Do you feel comfortable with the knowledge you have about you medical problems? What sort of clothes should you wear to simplify your physician's exam? What medications are you currently using, if any? Should your medicine be taken before the office visit? What specimens, if any, should you bring along? Should you wear make-up?

Learning About Your Medical Problems

In recent years many patients have visited my office with new information about their medical problems found through research at libraries, read in popular publications, or located over the Internet. This trend towards self-education is commendable. A patient should be as knowledgeable as possible about their problems. You should bring in questions you have written down and prioritized. According to Michele Greene, a researcher on doctor-patient communication associated with Brooklyn College, New York, "Bringing in a list of questions is really essential. And then [don't] be afraid to ask those questions." Studies indicate that doctors will better remember medical problems discussed by their assertive patients. Informed and assertive patients have better outcomes according to Debra Roter a behavioral scientist associated with Johns Hopkins University. Involved patients tend to understand their problems better and recall doctors instructions better according to an article by Linda Greider reported in *The Nation*, a news publication for AARP(American Association of Retired People) members.

In the appendix is a list of numerous health oriented Internet web sights that will provide the latest information on many of the medical problems you may be struggling with. Please use the available information to prepare for your office visit. **Good Hunting!**

What To Wear

Let's start with clothing. When patients select clothing that can be conveniently rearranged during a physical exam, it saves patients time, anxiety and effort. This point is especially important for handicapped and older patients, who may have difficulty changing clothes. No one, however, should be excluded from dressing appropriately. Patients often do not take into account the manner of their dress for medical examinations, so a few suggestions may be helpful. When possible, women should wear two-piece outfits to every medical appointment. Examination of the chest, back and abdomen is usually simplified by easily rearranging a shirt, blouse, sweater or pants when necessary. Clothing with buttons and zippers also lend themselves to physical examination. One-piece dresses are best left at home. Should you be seeing your physician for an injury or problem related to a lower extremity, tight jeans and snug pants should be avoided. Women should avoid wearing pantyhose when visiting their physician because the evaluation of many medical problems or injuries requires an examination of the lower extremities. Should you be wearing panty hose, they must often be removed to examine your lower extremities. Wearing underwear instead with calf high stockings will avoid the need to remove panty hose or undergarments. Weather permitting, shorts or skirts are often good choices, though loose fitting warm-up pants or slacks that can be easily lifted up above the knees are also acceptable. "Working women" should try to find a happy medium between the requirements of their job and the requirements of a physical examination.

How Should Children Dress?

Children and adolescents provide other problems that need to be considered for an office visit. Dressing conveniently is especially helpful when examining children and adolescents, who tend to be uncomfortable in gowns or covered with makeshift sheets or drapes. Many offices may lack gowns and accessories, complicating the examination process should your child not be conveniently dressed. Many adolescent girls like to wear turtleneck sweaters or turtleneck shirts to feel more comfortable in cold climates. These clothing items should be avoided whenever possible because they interfere with the examination of the neck, heart and upper chest. Try to anticipate what form of attire will lend itself best to the examination of your child. Correct dressing to minimize the removal of clothing will speed up the evaluation of a child and lessen their anxiety as well.

Medication Awareness

Awareness of your current medications is another important consideration. The National Academy of Sciences in 1999, reported that about 7,000 patients die annually due to medication errors. Most of these errors are avoidable when patients better understand their medical problems and how their medications work to manage their illnesses. A surprising number of patients are unfamiliar with their medication's name, dosage and frequency of use. This information is a necessary part of every office visit. Drug interactions and other side effects can occur if your physician adds additional medications to your regimen without a full understanding of your current treatment program.

Many people assume that their physician is already aware of medications they are using. Several situations may occur however, when your physician is not fully aware of your current prescription medication usage. For example, you may be using medication prescribed by another physician or specialist. You may be using medication given to you from a recent emergency room visit. Occasionally, you may be on medication that was phoned in after hours, and your office records may not be up-to-date. Sometimes medical records are misplaced, or they may even be inaccurate. Sometimes, pharmacists make prescription errors unbeknownst to you – giving out the wrong medication or an incorrect dosage. You may be taking medication prescribed by your previous primary care physician, and your old records have not been transferred or received by your new physician.

There are often instances when a patient is taken to an emergency room directly from work, and they may be unaware of their current medications – a situation which presents unnecessary problems for the emergency room physician. In fact, one of the most common reasons for going to an emergency room is to be evaluated for injuries after an automobile accident. If you are in a coma and unable to explain your current medication usage, problems may occur during your treatment. Carrying a list of medications in your purse or wallet can be of great help to a busy ER physician.

Over the years many patients have complained to me that they were never told by a previous physician the reason why a drug was prescribed for them. Some were told by their doctor, but do not remember what purpose the medication served. Always ask your physician to explain carefully why a medication has been prescribed and what its benefits may be. A category of drugs referred to as the beta-blockers are a good example of a commonly used class of medications that have multiple uses. They can be used to treat high blood pressure, reduce the frequency of palpitations (a feeling like an "extra heart beat"), eliminate or reduce the frequency of migraine headaches, and even in some cases assist in the management of heart failure. You can now see why adequate knowledge about your medications can prove to be very helpful ; if not mandatory when visiting with your physician. Try to learn the names of your medications and their intended use as it applies to your circumstances.

For all of the above reasons, it is important to have in your possession an accurate detailed list of current medications including the medication name, dosage, frequency of use, and intended use (the medical problem treated with each drug). Record this information in an organized fashion on a piece of paper. Carry this paper with you at all times and present it to any physician that you will be seeing at the start of your office visit. In fact, hand it to him as you sit down, even before he/she requests the information about your medication usage.

Please refer to the appendix for one possible way of organizing this information.

Withholding Medication

When should medication be withheld? Some patients wonder occasionally whether or not they should take their usual prescription medication before a medical office visit. Under most circumstances, patients should take their medications as prescribed. There are, however, a few common exceptions. Certain tests or studies can be affected by the ingestion of some medications. For example, ultrasound studies sometimes have to be canceled if a patient has ingested fluids or medication prior to their study. Some medications taken after certain tests can prove to be dangerous. For example, a commonly used medication for the treatment of diabetes – if taken shortly after tests utilizing intravenous dyes – may result in permanent kidney damage. On other occasions, some medicines work more effectively when taken with food and therefore should not be taken while fasting for a test. If one is fasting overnight, preparing for an early morning blood test, diabetic medications should be withheld. In fact, if a fasting diabetic patient takes insulin or some oral diabetic medication on an empty stomach, a dangerously low blood glucose level could occur, resulting in potentially serious consequences.

Another fairly common reason to temporarily hold or discontinue a medication relates to the performance of an exercise stress test. Some blood pressure or heart medications, when taken prior to an exercise test, will interfere with the interpretation of the test. On other occasions, withholding high blood pressure medications or certain heart medications can have adverse consequences. Usually blood pressure medication should be taken as prescribed, even when fasting for a test or special examination.

You should also make sure to take your blood pressure medication before an office visit intended to check your blood pressure. If you haven't taken your blood pressure medication before your visit, your physician may be unable to determine whether or not the medication you usually take is working properly. Blood pressure medication will not work longer then

85

twenty-four hours, so when not taken daily your blood pressure will rise above normal shortly after missing the next scheduled dose.

When in doubt about how, when, or where to take your medications, the best policy is to call your physician's office the day before a medical test or office visit to clarify whether or not your medication should be taken or withheld.

Final Preparations

Bathing before an examination is also worthwhile. Before an office visit, avoid exercising unless you are able to shower immediately afterwards. Health care workers appreciate efforts towards cleanliness, especially when dealing with children. Deodorant should not be worn before a mammography because it may interfere with your evaluation.

Should you be visiting your doctor to have a rash or acne evaluated, avoid wearing makeup, creams, lotions or homemade concoctions that may alter one's physical appearance. Accurate diagnosis can be hampered by self-medication just before an office visit. Avoid wearing nail polish, since by covering up your nail beds you may eliminate some clues helpful to diagnosing a variety of unwanted conditions.

Occasionally patients are anxious before some sensitive examinations. Pelvic examinations for some, sigmoidoscopies (see glossary) for others, and often MRIs for many can prove to be quite anxiety-provoking. If you fall into any of the above categories, diazepam (Valium) exhibits three very useful properties. It works as a muscle relaxer, an antispasmodic, and an anxiety-relieving medication, all very useful benefits when taken thirty to sixty minutes before a worrisome or uncomfortable examination. In my experience, Valium is especially helpful when given to patients one hour preceding the examination of their lower bowel or rectum with a flexible sigmoidoscope. For many patients, this medication will prevent spasms and cramping within the lower colon and abdomen, easing the exam considerably. Many of my patients have been pleased by the beneficial effects of these medicines when used occasionally prior to some unpleasant test or procedure. Make sure to discuss your anxieties about an exam with your physician; he or she may be able to prescribe a medication that will make the exam easier. For some patients, these medications may cause drowsiness; you may, therefore, want to ask a friend or relative to provide transportation to and from your office visit.

Chapter 17

The Day of Your Office Visit

Eventually, the day for your medical appointment arrives. Before leaving your home or place of work, it may be helpful to call your doctor's office to verify if he is running on time. This serves two useful purposes. One, it allows for last-minute scheduling corrections, which may benefit you if an unforeseen problem arises. On rare occasions, two patients have been scheduled for the same appointment time. Therefore, calling in advance may allow for adjustments when necessary. Secondly, it puts the office on notice that your time is valuable. For most patients, waiting one to two hours for a medical visit is not acceptable, and it may be prevented by simply calling ahead to verify the status of your appointment.

Once your appointment has been verified, try to arrive on time or even a few minutes early. Occasionally, you may be rewarded for your timeliness when another patient cancels or does not arrive. This scenario is not rare; it generally happens several times per day.

After arriving at your doctor's office, always check in. Many managed care plans require each patient to pay a copay of $5 - $20 at the time of each office visit before services are provided. Arriving early would be an ideal time to pay your copay with cash or check. Should this be your first appointment when visiting a new physician, time will be required for the completion of forms that provide appropriate medical insurance information: your place of employment, responsible friends or relatives to be contacted in the event of an emergency, your social security number, and current home and work phone numbers. Other facts such as family history may also be requested.

While waiting to see your doctor, avoid using the bathroom without checking with a nurse or receptionist first. Often a urine specimen is needed for diagnostic purposes and wasting it may require another trip back to your physician's office or local laboratory.

If you have been sitting in the waiting room for fifteen minutes or longer without being called back to be seen, return to the receptionist and inquire about the status of your appointment. This maneuver is especially wise if other patients arriving after your scheduled time have been taken back ahead of you. Occasionally, mistakes occur and patients are taken back out of sequence. Also, if several physicians are seeing patients at the same time, patients can be lost in the shuffle. Regrettably, this has happened in my office on several occasions.

If you have another engagement scheduled after your office visit – a waiting child to be picked up or an airplane to catch, for instance – it's best to alert the office staff of these needs upon arrival, so that you're kept on schedule. After all, what are schedules for?

Chapter 18

The Wait

Your time is a precious commodity, and most offices try to reduce your waiting time. Some offices, however, do not understand this concept. Excessive waiting on a routine basis indicates poor office management, insensitivity, selfishness, or all of the above. In primary care offices, long wait times are only rarely due to emergencies, despite what many patients have been told. Yes, some patients' problems may be more complicated than anticipated, but experienced physicians usually should be able to keep reasonably close to a time schedule. One or two hour waits should happen only rarely, if at all. If you are forced into long waits regularly, you may want to find medical care elsewhere. Careful, thoughtful office scheduling is not rocket science. It simply involves common sense and adequate consideration of each patients' needs. Fortunately, managed care organizations are monitoring waiting times in physicians' offices – resulting in better service and streamlined care.

Chapter 19

Waiting Rooms: An Opportunity for Reflection

Unfortunately, we all know what it is like to sit and wait in a waiting room. Doctors' offices top the list for record-breaking waits, though most physicians today are attempting to alleviate this chronic irritation and to improve patient satisfaction. If your attempts at proper appointment scheduling fail to prevent this problem, be prepared to make the most of your wait.

Waiting rooms can provide useful opportunities to review your thoughts. Reconsider why you are visiting your physician. Review mentally how you will present your symptoms or describe your problem. Carefully think through when your illness began, what are its most uncomfortable aspects and what you have already tried to do to solve or relieve your problem. Formulate a list of questions to review if you have not already done so. Never be afraid to ask questions nor discuss fears you may harbor about your health. An old Danish proverb reminds us, "He who is afraid to ask is ashamed of learning."

In addition, some medical visits require patient completion of various forms to provide additional information. For example, you may be required to fill out a comprehensive medical history form revealing not only your past medical history but also important medical problems of close family members. Some information such as immunization records available from a previous physician may be required for completeness. Medical records kept at home may assist you in providing needed information. Bringing along these records for your initial office visit will aid in completing forms provided by your new physician's office staff. If this task was not completed at home where records may be available, then do the best you can to fill out pertinent information while waiting.

There are many other important health related forms for children and adults that should be at least partially completed before the scheduled office visit. Children are confronted with forms for camping trips, school trips, and athletics. Other students bring along forms required for admission to public schools, colleges or universities. The upper part of each form will have spaces for a patient's name, address, phone numbers, and past medical history (when required). These portions of the form should be filled out before a patient sees their physician.

Schools also require a current list of medications that your child may need administered during routine school hours. One of the more frequent drugs given on a regular basis to students is Ritalin, usually dispensed during the lunch hour to children with attention deficit disorder. Your school is interested in the name of each medication, its dosage, frequency of use and common side effects. You must fill out this form completely and accurately. If you do not correctly complete your portion of the school form, your physician will be unable to sign off on it using your valuable appointment time to do so.

A wide variety of documents brought into the office include forms for workman's compensation, accidents, disability, exercise clubs, return to work papers, pre-school teacher evaluation forms and various government reports. One problem common to most of these forms is that patients have failed to complete the sections of the form pertaining to personal information. Waiting time may be available to carefully fill out these forms if you not have completed them at home.

If your children are of school age and have homework requirements, bringing it along to your doctor's office may prove useful should waiting be necessary. Younger children often like to bring along small hand-held computer games which, when operational, tend to create any number of strange sounds and beeps. Please ask your children when necessary to be considerate of others whenever possible.

In summary, waiting time may present a terrific opportunity to psychologically prepare to speak and visit with your physician. *Do your part in preparing for a valuable as well as educational experience.*

Chapter 20

Tools of the Trade

During your office visit, educational tools, questionnaires, prescriptions and possibly the use of medical appliances are discussed. For example, some patients suffering from headaches are asked to take home a headache questionnaire to fill out. Upon their return visit, this form if carefully filled out will assist their doctor in diagnosing the cause of their headaches. Some patients may be given educational materials such as diet instruction sheets, back exercise sheets, or other instructional materials. It is wise to review this information shortly after your visit when the issues are fresh in your mind.

Sometimes physicians or nurses promise to give patients some form of instructional or educational materials at the end of a visit and then forget to do so. Don't hesitate to request what was promised to you should your physician forget. In busy offices, these spells of forgetfulness can happen, especially when the materials are not located right in the exam room. It's also easy for your doctor to forget these items if he or she is interrupted for an emergency or an important phone call. We are human and make mistakes, but patients should not be embarrassed to ask for what was offered.

Prescriptions are the most common items given to patients before leaving – and often several of them at that. Count your prescriptions. Review the names of the medicines. Some medications are listed by their brand name, while others are listed by their generic name. HMOs sometimes accidentally switch medications with names that sound similar, but are in fact different. Check the names on the bottles against your own list to be sure all of your prescriptions were written correctly. When looking at your prescriptions, check to see if refills were ordered. Check the strength or dosage of the medication as well.

Occasionally, your physician's records may not be current. Sometimes medications were phoned in during evenings when the office was closed, and no record of the new dosage or

95

medication appears in your current medical record. Your doctor may have handled many phone calls after hours and will not realize what transpired unless he kept accurate records of the phone calls. Any help you can provide in verifying the names and dosages of medications phoned in after hours may be very helpful. Carefully reviewing your new prescriptions before leaving can prevent extra work on everyone's part. Patients who never become familiar with their medications risk a number of problems and complications.

Before leaving, some patients will request that a nurse phone in their prescriptions to a local pharmacy to reduce their waiting time when they arrive. Some ask that medications be rewritten on special forms that can be faxed immediately to an out of town pharmacy. Whenever possible, your physician's staff will accommodate these requests. However, cost cutbacks related to lower physician reimbursement from insurance companies has resulted in lower levels of office staffing. Your physician's staff may be so time-constricted that they may not always be able to honor your request. Pharmacies also suffer from limited staffing and sometimes place medical assistants on hold for dreadful periods of time. When your doctor's office appears to be less busy than usual, the staff will often be happy to accommodate your prescription requests.

What about specific appliances or devices that may have been given to you for use? Were you given adequate instruction by your doctor or his nurse on how to use them? A common example of a somewhat difficult device to use is a metered dose inhaler, or "puffer," carried by many asthmatic patients. If your puffer is not properly used or activated when you're inhaling, the medication will not be fully deposited in your lungs. It's been my experience that the majority of patients fail to use inhalers properly. Misunderstandings associated with equipment use is common place. If you do not have a clear understanding of how to use any device, ask for more instruction.

Many other pieces of medical equipment might be given to you to assist your recovery. Commonly used devices could include a wrist splint for carpal tunnel syndrome, an air cast for a sprained ankle, a cervical neck collar for a neck injury, a Reese

96

Boot for foot pain, and so on. Each piece of equipment must be used according to proper guidelines to achieve optimum results. Understand their use, and if you don't, do not be afraid to ask questions. Don't be shy. The lack of proper patient education is an area of weakness that could be improved upon in many medical offices. You deserve good care and proper education, so demand it in a pleasant way if it hasn't been provided. Many patients struggle with all sorts of problems that were overlooked or forgotten. Get your money's worth. A little extra time and education will improve your level of satisfaction and will improve your chances of an uneventful recovery.

Chapter 21

Who Should Accompany a Patient?

Generally, when a competent adult patient visits a physician, no one else needs to attend. There are, of course, exceptions to this rule – some of which will be addressed shortly. Usually, communication between a physician and his patient occurs best when they are alone and in a small, quiet exam room. Some patients wish to see their doctor with their spouse or significant other. For some, this arrangement is helpful or even necessary. However, it may often prove detrimental to the doctor-patient relationship, and therefore it is not always in one's best interests. Some spouses can present very helpful information, but on occasion, their presence can be counterproductive and actually stifle conversation that may be considered personal by the patient. As a patient, whether or not someone accompanies you to an office visit is a personal decision that you alone must make.

You have experienced the illness, and no matter how helpful someone else wishes to be, they may be hindering rather then helping the process along. Only the patient really knows how a particular symptom or problem has affected his or her body or life. Only a patient actually knows when symptoms occur, how severe they are, how long they last and how they feel. A caring friend or spouse may realize when their significant other appears to be sick or "out of sorts," but since they have not experienced the actual symptoms themselves they really are not able to express the true essence of a problem.

When trying to speak for a patient, a patient's advocate may provide inaccurate or unnecessary information. They may unintentionally dominate an interview, allowing less time for a physician to find out from the patient accurate details that may shed light on their illness. When it appears that the patient is competent and trustworthy, his or her information is generally the most helpful and reliable. Second-hand information is often inaccurate.

Sometimes, however, a friend or spouse can provide quality information that a patient otherwise may not reveal. Collaboration between a physician and a significant other may be valuable. The physician must always respect the confidentiality of a patient's problem during these discussions. It's also wise on most occasions not to reveal sources of information provided by a co-operative relative or friend, thereby possibly disturbing their relationship. Most patients do not wish to have others meddle in their affairs, but in the case of the very old, the incompetent, or the seriously ill, it can be in a patient's best interest for others to provide information.

As demonstrated by the following example it may be helpful to have more than one caregiver in attendance during some painful discussions. In reference to her sickly father, a patient of mine commented not too long age, "My dad was in his 70's and he had congestive heart failure. My sister and my mother and I were there. We heard different things. There are trigger words you hear and once you hear them you don't hear anything else. When I heard congestive heart failure I didn't hear anything after that."

Patient Compentency

There are frequent situations in which the competency of a patient may be called into question. "Common law dictates that individuals possess autonomy and self-determination, which emcompass the right to accept or refuse medical treatment....Our legal system endorses the principle that all persons are competent to make reasoned decisions unless demonstrated to be otherwise." (*Primary Care Companion Journal Of Clinical Psychiatry*, 1999; 1:131-141).

Sometimes physicians may believe a patient to be incompetent should they refuse a recommended treatment. This position is often inaccurate on both legal and moral grounds. Patients have a right to make choices good, bad, and otherwise unless they have been found to be incompetent based on past decisions or laws tested by our judicial system. Three standards may be used to evaluate a patient's competence; goal directed thinking, a functional memory, and acceptable as opposed to bizarre behavior. Other criteria of competence would include the ability to make a decision and then to express an opinion about their decision. One must also be able to understand what options they may have available to them. Patients lacking a sound memory or sufficient intelligence may not be able to understand their options. Some patients may not be able to comprehend what effects a treatment may have on them, be the effects good or bad. These patients may also be incompetent. Patients have the right to refuse any treatment they wish as long as their physician believes their patient understands the consequences of whatever decision they make.

Should a patient be found to be incompetent by the courts or should they convey their rights to a friend or relative (surrogate) then the surrogate must act on the patients behalf. A surrogate's choice in managing their patient's medical affairs would be based on what they believe their patient would have chosen if they were of sound mind. Not knowing that, the surrogate's choice would be based on what any reasonable person would have chosen under similar circumstances.

One of the best examples of an incompetent patient is someone suffering from Alzheimer's disease. These patients require someone else to speak for them and manage their affairs, be them medical or otherwise.

Some patients have prepared living wills or advanced directives. Unfortunately experience has shown that they have often not discussed their thoughts or desires with either family members or their physician. Patients or their surrogates should be as well prepared as possible to discuss their medical needs with their physician. This will result in the highest level of patient satisfaction.

Presenting the Facts to Your Physician

Whenever possible, each patient must be willing to provide clear facts to assist their physician in diagnosing his or her problem. On occasion, you may not know which facts to provide to your doctor, or how to provide them. It then becomes the responsibility of your doctor to ask leading and pointed questions. It may take several office visits before a patient feels comfortable enough with their physician to provide sensitive information that could prove embarrassing or frightening. When possible, write down on paper your complaints or symptoms before an office visit. Think through your illness, preparing to present the facts of your problem as carefully as possible. Your physician wants to help but must be armed with the facts – as difficult or as painful as they may be. Providing good medical care always begins with an accurate and complete history.

You may sometimes struggle when presenting your problem. Generally, an experienced physician can tell when an anxious or depressed patient is not providing a complete picture. Over time, each physician must try to win over his patient's confidence. The sooner a satisfactory comfort level between you and your doctor can be reached, the quicker good results may be achieved. If you don't feel comfortable discussing your problems with your physician, consider changing doctors.

Patients are sometimes embarrassed by certain unhealthy habits or relationships, and they therefore choose not to comment on them. They may neglect to mention key problems, such as spousal abuse, drug abuse or alcohol abuse. They may underestimate their smoking habit or deny overeating difficulties. They may ignore child abuse, job stress and other volatile emotional problems. Here is where a spouse or friend can provide helpful information should a patient's history be lacking. There are ways that a motivated physician can obtain an accurate medical history without violating patient-doctor confidentiality.

The Fearful Adolescent

"The great advantage of telling the truth is that one's so much more likely to sound convincing."
- **Susan Howatch,**
Absolute Truths

On occasion, an uncooperative adolescent patient has been dragged against their will into a physician's office by a worried parent. These situations are difficult, and a physician must handle them carefully. Sometimes it may be difficult to determine who the real patient is.

A memorable experience occurred in the early 1970s when I was serving as a general medical officer with the U. S. Army at Fort Lee, Virginia. At that stage in my career, I was relatively inexperienced, naive and a little too trusting of patient information. One afternoon, a sixteen-year-old girl, accompanied by her parents, came in to see me for evaluation of a mysterious abdominal mass. After questioning the frightened adolescent and later examining her, I noted what I believed to be a pregnancy of four- or five-months' gestation. Asking the parents to leave, I questioned the patient vigorously on the issue of sexual intercourse, but she profusely denied that she had ever experienced anything of the sort. Even after I revealed my concern that she was probably pregnant, she still denied the possibility. Although I confronted her with the fact that I suspected she was not being completely honest, she nonetheless stuck to her story. Eventually, she convinced me that she was telling the truth, and I then feared the worst – possibly cancer or an ovarian tumor. I decided to obtain an abdominal x-ray to assist in my diagnosis, though x-rays are usually not recommended during pregnancy except under unusual circumstances. In those days, ultrasound technology was not as available as it is today. She had won over my trust, and though urine pregnancy tests were available in the 1970s, I didn't order one. After I viewed the x-ray results, however, the truth finally surfaced. She was carrying a four- or five-month-old fetus. In this case, the frightened young lady was so fearful of her parents' possible negative reactions that she could still not bring herself to admit the truth. Ever since that experience, I have looked at some of my patients with healthy skepticism. When a patient is fearful or anxious, ferreting out the facts can be challenging.

Children

Children can present their physician with other challenges. For medical and legal reasons, children must be accompanied by a parent or legal guardian to receive medical care. When this is not possible, written permission from a parent or legal guardian allowing their child to be treated by a physician is usually acceptable. If the adult accompanying a child lacks a full understanding of the child's illness, he or she should have a written description from a knowledgeable party detailing any facts pertaining to the child's office visit. When an older sibling or an adult lacking legal custody accompanies a minor, they should bring along a permission slip from a parent or legal guardian allowing a physician to provide care. They should also have a note from a knowledgeable parent or caregiver describing symptoms and information that may prove useful in the care of the child. The person accompanying the child must also be aware of any of the child's drug allergies and current medications. Please see Appendix A.

Upon questioning by an experienced physician, younger children are often reliable historians who can provide good information about their problems. In contrast, teenagers can be reluctant to reveal comprehensive details about their symptoms or illness. In this case, the physician must extract relevant details through clever and persistent questioning. Even then, facts provided by some adolescents can sometimes remain skimpy, resulting in an incomplete care plan. It is often helpful for an informed adult to accompany minors to assist in providing information to the physician. This is not necessary in every case. Many adolescents are perfectly capable of handling their own affairs in an accurate and honest way. A physician should respect an adolescent's privacy on confidential matters when the adolescent chooses. Dealing with adolescents must be founded on trust to achieve the highest degree of success.

Most parents have a fairly good idea of how their children will perform when visiting their physician. Parents should, however, be careful not to dominate the visit. Heavy-handed tactics may cause hard feelings later on. Prior to an office visit, it may be useful for a parent to coach their child about providing clear answers and helpful information to their doctor during the medical evaluation.

Sometimes children and teenagers are reluctant to fully cooperate when it comes to a physical examination. In recent years, many children have been schooled by their parents to never allow anyone to touch or view their "private parts." Often I hear parents say, "It's okay, he's a doctor."

Prior to an office visit, parents should mentally prepare their child for some form of physical examination by discussing with them what may be done. If the exam is done properly, a child's fears can be lessened. By the same token, a physician should respect their patients' privacy as much as clinically possible, examining them conservatively and limiting exposure of sensitive areas. Should examination of the genital or breast area be necessary, the physician should use the utmost discretion. Often a nurse or medical assistant can be present during the exam to assist or comfort a nervous patient. If as a parent you're aware of your child's fear about the exam, discuss this problem with your child's physician in advance so extra care may be provided. Do not hesitate to request that a nurse assist your physician if you feel that the extra assistance would benefit your child.

Many children respond much better to a physician who speaks softly and directly. Too many physicians ask the parent all of their questions, never addressing the child. This oversight may result in a lack of trust and cooperation from the child. If your doctor falls into this category, mention to him or her that your child is capable of answering most of the questions. If your child flounders or talks excessively, then assist him or her in getting back on track. Finally, if after repeated visits your doctor doesn't seem to work well with your child, consider looking for one more skilled in the art of child evaluation and management. Sometimes one has to visit several physicians to find a doctor who best suits their family's needs.

One other common problem in child or adolescent care is the need to use injections as part of an office visit. Preparing your child in advance can help prevent struggles in the exam room. Sometimes, firmness on the part of a parent is the only solution. A physician rarely can be convincing if a parent is unsupportive or unwilling to exert proper authority.

Chapter 22

Patients Requiring Assistance

The Examination of Children

The physical examination of children is associated with its own unique set of challenges. However, contrary to popular belief, the examination of a child is no more difficult than that of anyone else and is actually much less complicated. Winning the child over by eliminating or reducing fear is the key to a successful and uneventful exam. A parent should play a big role in this arena if optimum results are hoped for.

Prior to an office visit, a parent should explain to their child the benefits of the medical visit. Each visit has its own set of benefits, and, depending on a child's age, he or she may understand this if an enthusiastic parent presents it.

It's often best to bring in your child for a well visit to first introduce them to their new doctor in a non-threatening way. This visit should simply be a "get-acquainted visit" and should not be associated with injections or any other uncomfortable maneuvers. Putting your child at ease early during the doctor-patient experience is the key to long-term success.

Because examinations can be unsettling to some children, they need to be conducted in a non-frightening way. When a child has been previously mishandled during an exam with unnecessary restraints, over-aggressive use of a tongue depressor or careless use of an ear otoscope, children may remain frightened of medical personnel for years to come.

If your child is terribly frightened of doctors from earlier difficult experiences, it is best to share this information with your physician to help prepare him or her to work with your child in a non-threatening way. Hopefully, a well-informed physician will then take additional time and care when working with your child; thus reducing the chance of another unpleasant experience. As a parent, you can play a major role in reducing your child's fear.

The best way to examine a younger child is for a parent to sit on the examination table holding the child in her arms. Proper positioning of your child will make your child more comfortable and will allow you to assist your physician during the examination. After taking a seat on the exam table, place your child sideways on your lap with their legs draped either over or between yours. Then rest their shoulder against your chest. This comfortable position allows your child to be held while seeing you and permits the doctor to examine your child's back, hopefully with a warmed stethoscope. Examining a child's back first is non-threatening and easily accomplished by lifting up the back of their shirt or blouse. Next their chest and heart can be checked while you are closely holding your child in a reassuring way. Examining less sensitive areas initially will allow your child to develop trust with the examining physician.

Patient's ears being more sensitive can be examined next. Children's ears are best examined by repositioning your child so they are facing you; have them face you while placing their legs around your waist. Then gently turn your child's face to one side or the other and rest their head against your chest. In this position, your doctor will easily be able to look into one of your child's ears using an otoscope. Then turn your child's head to the other side again resting their head on your chest allowing your doctor to check the other ear. This process nearly always goes smoothly and permits good control of your child's head with both of your hands should the need arise.

It's now time to examine your child's abdomen. The abdomen can sometimes be adequately examined while being held in an upright position should your child be frightened of lying down; a frequent problem. Some kids refuse to lie down on an exam table. When a parent stands near the exam table holding their child's hand or placing their cheek on theirs, it will relieve their child's anxiety during the examination. Examining a child's abdomen can also sometimes be a challenge for other reasons. Many children are ticklish and find the exam to be amusing, making them laugh and tightening their stomach muscles. Under these circumstances, your doctor will find it difficult to gain useful information. If you know that your child tends to be ticklish, please *do not* mention this problem within earshot of your child prior to the abdominal exam. It will *always* and without exception result in a giggling child, reducing the chance of an informative abdominal examination. Give your doctor a fighting chance by not mentioning out loud that your child is ticklish. When all else fails, a ticklish stomach can be overcome by having your child press downward on the top of your doctor's hands during the abdominal examination. This will eliminate the ticklish feeling and will allow for at least a marginal exam.

Once in a while, it is necessary during a physical exam to examine a child's genital area. This can be alarming to some children, especially when parents have warned them never to allow anyone to touch their genital area. It is important for parents to discuss with their children not only it is okay, but it is sometimes necessary, to have their genital area checked during an examination by a physician or a nurse. Children must be assured that they will not be harmed during the exam. Having this talk with your child before their office visit may prevent a scene if you suspect an exam of this type may be necessary.

The very last part of a child's exam – and often the most difficult – involves the evaluation of their mouth and throat. Many children have been frightened in the past by overly aggressive use of a tongue depressor and can therefore be uncooperative. This problem can be reduced by parental assistance and gentle persuasion on the part of your physician. First, it is good to remember that your child's throat is best examined when they are placed in an upright position, seated on your lap and looking straight ahead at their physician. When assisting your physician, you can gain further control of your child by resting their back against your chest. This position will keep your child facing forward, which will make your doctor's evaluation easier. In this position, you will also be able to place your hands and forearms under your child's armpits. Next, reaching upward, you will be able to gently grasp your child's face, propping it forward and upward. Your doctor can then, with a little coaching, peer inside your child's open mouth – often without the use of a tongue depressor. When asked gently, a child will usually open his or her mouth widely, especially if the doctor is not holding a tongue depressor. Using a tongue depressor as briefly as possible, and only as a last resort, may still be necessary in order to examine your child's throat.

When your child is sitting upright and on your lap, gagging is greatly reduced. The problem of lung aspiration (choking on ones own secretions) is more likely to occur while a child is lying on his back across an exam table. This practice should be avoided whenever possible.

Examination of an older child is easier, but no less anxiety-provoking for your child. Parents should remain present during the exam of an older child unless the child prefers that their parent leave the room for a brief time during the examination of one's breasts or genital areas.   Parents may feel most comfortable looking away during some examinations, but their presence is often appreciated by all concerned.

Parents can be very helpful during a child's physical exam and are encouraged to participate to the degree that they are facilitating the process.

After the evaluation has been completed, parents and children should feel free to ask any questions they may have concerning their office visit. Questions may be directed at all aspects of the visit from testing to treatment as well as the proper use of medication.

Avoidable Examination Room Problems:

On several occasions, I have had a well-intentioned parent come into my office with a screaming or misbehaving child. In hopes of settling their child down, I have heard parents comment, "If you don't quiet down, the doctor will give you a shot." This approach is unacceptable for several reasons. First, a physician's role is not one of a disciplinarian. That is a parental responsibility. Secondly, this type of comment is intended to instill a sense of fear within a child, implying that a physician intends to hurt or harm them rather than to help or comfort them.

Parents should have only one child at a time in an exam room whenever possible. Two or more children in the same room usually results in excessive talking, playing, noise and commotion from their interactions or attempts to compete for attention. It's easier for physicians to diagnose and treat medical problems when the atmosphere is subdued.

Many medical offices that treat children now have play areas where siblings can be left. For a brief period of time, office personnel can keep a watchful eye on children. If, however, you're able to find a babysitter or an extra hand, your physician will be grateful, and so will your other children.

Likewise, when adults are scheduled to see their physician, they should not bring children along during their office visit. Whenever possible make other arrangements. When children are brought along, they will often prove to be a distraction, both to the parent as well as to the physician. I have often felt that noisy or playful children can interfere with clear or expedient thinking. Time spent correcting children interferes with the flow of the evaluation and results in less time available for a quality office visit.

Some parents also erroneously believe it is acceptable to bring children along with them if the child brings along toys for entertainment purposes. Children often do not use toys in their intended manner. Instead, they are often used as hammers against chairs, walls, tables or doctors. If one brings a child with them to an office visit, it's best to leave their toys at home, with the possible exception of blankets or stuffed animals. In my experience, it is usually easier to deal with toyless children who then tend to watch the evaluation rather than create distractions. At any rate, when possible, leave the kids at home.

On occasion, teenagers will bring along a friend or companion to an office visit. This practice is generally not advisable, since it will often limit conversation on sensitive issues. Should a teenager bring along a friend, it is best to have their friend remain in the waiting room during the evaluation.

If patients and physicians feel it's mutually beneficial, then it is acceptable to move parents, relatives or friends back and forth between exam and waiting rooms as circumstances dictate to provide optimum medical care. However, the less time spent in juggling the exam room's inhabitants, the better.

111

The Use Of A Chaperone During a Female Exam

Another important consideration pertaining to women and adolescents is the presence of a chaperone in the exam room during a female examination. If it increases a woman's comfort level, patients are encouraged to request that a nurse or similar assistant be in attendance for examinations should the physician not routinely provide this service. Doctors are generally receptive to any patient's requests that increase their comfort or security levels. It is of interest to note that on rare occasions some women prefer not to have a chaperone in attendance. Once again, personal preferences are the key to remember during any physical evaluation and should be voiced to your physician as you see fit. Some physicians always insist on chaperones for nearly any form of examination to discourage lawsuits from patients who may attempt false accusations for financial gain.

Adolescents should be dressed in two-piece outfits to minimize the need to remove clothing, thereby allowing for either partially lifting or lowering a garment as needed to expose the area in question. Being conveniently dressed for an exam will result in less rather than more exposure, reducing both your doctor's work and a patient's anxiety level.

Other Special Cases:

A situation that bears some discussion is the evaluation of an adult or child who is intellectually or psychologically disabled. Whenever possible, they should be accompanied by a responsible adult who best understands their needs and problems.

With a little extra effort on the part of family members, friends and your physician, these patients need not be difficult to care for. They may, however, exhibit more fear and anxiety than others in their age group, and therefore, additional time is usually warranted for careful evaluation. Also, if the guardian of an intellectually challenged individual does not accompany the patient to the doctor's office, a permission slip must accompany

112

them. This same policy holds true for children under the age of eighteen not accompanied by a parent or guardian. If a well-informed adult cannot be in attendance, a thorough note listing the patient's needs or problems should accompany them. For an example of a permission form, see Appendix A at the end of the book.

Physicians will occasionally evaluate patients that are speech or hearing-impaired. A parent, friend or interested party accompanying the patient and familiar with their problems can be a great asset. When alone, these patients are more likely to experience problems when dealing with the health care system. As you already know, fully-functional adults have enough problems of their own in dealing with the system, let alone children or handicapped adults. Many hearing-impaired patients do quite well with lip-reading and are able to handle themselves adequately without additional assistance.

Some patients do not speak the language of their chosen physician. This scenario can lead to many problems, including inaccurate history-taking, misunderstandings, wrong diagnoses, the misuse of medication or the incorrect use of other therapeutic modalities. These problems are usually avoidable. Bringing along a translator may seem adequate, but little nuances in any given language can have an altogether different meaning – resulting in confusion on the part of both the patient and the physician. Many concepts or complaints can be lost in translation. Whenever possible, one should visit a physician who is fluent in their own language. Not to do so may compromise one's medical care. We are all painfully aware of the fact that even when physicians and patients speak the same language, there are still frequent misunderstandings.

The Medical Record is Secret – Or is It??

Patients sometimes ask that certain facts be removed from their medical record. Other patients ask that certain facts or medical problems not be placed in their medical record. It is best for patients to use common sense and care in the discussion of medical problems with their physician during their visit.

113

Many physicians often begin writing a patient's comments in their medical record as the patient is presenting their symptoms. Once items are placed in the medical record, they cannot be removed or altered – this practice is considered unacceptable and even fraudulent. On occasion, you may wish to appraise your physician about very confidential issues, yet not have them written in your record. Should that be your need, mention to your doctor *before* presenting your case that you do not want your comments to become a matter of record. Your doctor will usually respect your wishes for privacy.

The proper handling of confidential affairs leads to a trusting relationship between physician and patient. Confidentiality is an absolute must in the doctor-patient relationship and can only be breached by a court order except under the most unusual of circumstances. However, one should keep in mind, in order to obtain or change medical insurances and life insurance policies, patients must often agree to submit to medical record review. Insurance companies usually look for preexisting conditions to adjust rates or even to refuse coverage. This practice by insurance companies, however, may eventually be stopped since new legislation protecting patients' rights is on the horizon.

Chapter 23

Useful Information to Bring Along to any Physician Visit

There are several items that a well-prepared patient should bring with them each time they visit any physician, whether it be their primary care physician or a specialist. Following these recommendations will give your physician and his office staff a good start in dealing with any problem you may have. Always bring the following items when visiting a physician:

1) Your medical insurance card and a current medical insurance manual.

These items provide information about hospitals, specialists, and laboratory or x-ray facilities that you may be referred to for evaluation, treatment or testing. Knowing which hospitals you may go to for urgent care and testing is important in today's age of managed care. Visiting the wrong hospitals or specialists can prove expensive if they are not covered under your health plan.

Each year there may be changes in your health care plan. Physicians may not renew their contracts. New specialists may be added to your plan. Hospitals may be added or discontinued. The delivery of health care is in a constant state of flux. A little forethought and preparation will go a long way in reducing confusion and will allow for improved service and care.

Patients often erroneously believe that their physician's office staff is familiar with all insurance plans. Due to the existence of numerous insurance products, along with annual policy changes, a reliable insurance manual is necessary to provide appropriate answers to even routine problems. Even current manuals are not always entirely up-to-date. They are however the best we have to work with.

Medical insurance plans are often customized to each employer, and therefore, benefits and options can vary widely from company to company. Without bringing along one's insurance manual for review, delays are often incurred.

2) A current list of any and all drugs to which you may be allergic or sensitive.

Each patient should carry with them at all times a list of any medications they have experienced problems with in the past. For example, if you are allergic to penicillin, as indicated by the onset of hives after having last taken it, you should record on your list the exact reaction that occurred. If you have had a rash due to a medication, record the details about the rash next to the name of the drug that caused it.

Side effects – as opposed to allergic reactions – are another matter altogether. Some people for example, may experience severe stomach distress with the use of codeine. Others may experience lightheadedness, abdominal cramps or any number of other symptoms referred to as side effects. Should these or other symptoms occur with any medication, it would be advisable to record these problems as side effects. It is important to record the exact reaction, because many side effects do not necessarily preclude the use of a drug. Providing accurate information to your physician reduces the chance of prescribing similar medications with adverse side effects. Carrying a list of medications and adverse drug reactions with you at all times will also be helpful in an emergency. Later on more information will be provided about drug allergies and side effects.

3) A list of current medication usage.

Many patients are currently taking prescription drugs prescribed by previous family physicians or specialists. Patients frequently do not know the names or dosages of their medication. This seems to be the rule rather than the exception. It is a big help to your physician when you are able to hand over an accurate list of medications that you are currently using. Your list should include the name of the drug, dosage, and number of times per day the medication is required.

To complicate the picture further, many patients do not understand the purpose or use of the medication they are taking. Many medicines have a variety of different uses for totally unrelated conditions. Knowing the intended use or purpose of each of your drugs is important to any physician who did not prescribe them. If your new physician requires changes in the use of your medications, he will be better equipped to do so if he has a clear picture of your needs. Therefore, on your list of medications also record the diagnosis or reason for each medication that you use. Please include the date the medication was started.

4) A brief medical and surgical history.

Many patients have complicated medical or surgical histories. A well-prepared patient will also carry a complete list of past surgeries and important medical problems that they are currently being treated for. Next to each surgery and medical problem, include the year that the problem was treated or diagnosed. For example, a patient might carry with them a form we could refer to as a Medical Information Form (See Appendix B). As one can see, a simple laundry list of important facts can be very helpful and provide a brief medical synopsis without the need of carrying old medical records from place to place. Medical records can be acquired when more details are required upon request of your doctor.

In summary, carrying a brief list of your medications, known drug allergies, side effects, and a list of chronic medical as well as past surgical problems will provide quick access to important information that will be helpful to medical personnel at your PCP's office, a specialist's office, or at the emergency room. This information will prove especially helpful when medical records have been misplaced or are not conveniently available. This synopsis of information will also provide a quick overview of your health and reduce the number of questions a physician will have to ask at the start of the interview, allowing more time for the primary reason of your visit. Please see appendix for examples of several useful forms.

Chapter 24

The Exam Room: Vital Signs and Measurements
Are Vital

After you have completed appropriate paperwork and forms in a satisfactory manner, it's time to be placed in an exam or consultation room. Patients are often weighed and measured before being placed in a room, though the need for these measurements will vary with circumstances and are not necessary at every visit. Likewise, appropriate vital signs such as temperature, blood pressure and pulse may be taken but may not be necessary with each visit.

Many patients, out of embarrassment or for personal reasons, often refuse to be weighed. However, weight changes – either loss or gain – can be very helpful in assessing one's general health. Many diseases or adverse conditions often influence a patient's weight.

It is also valuable for a physician to know if your weight has remained stable. Stable weight is often a sign of good health. Refusing to be weighed can delay the diagnosis or proper management of many serious or life-threatening conditions. Weight can fluctuate adversely with heart or kidney disease, cancer, tuberculosis, diabetes, thyroid disorders and dozens of other conditions. Some patients routinely refuse to allow an assistant to weigh them. Sometimes your physician will request your weight later on when he notes that it hasn't been recorded in your record. I have rarely had a patient refuse to be weighed after they have received a reasonable explanation for the need to measure it.

With some eating disorders it's best not to weigh a patient before each visit. When necessary, weighing some patients should be done discretely since knowledge of their weight may affect them emotionally, resulting in adverse outcomes. When it's preferable for a patient not to know their exact weight, they should be asked to face backwards on the scale during their measurement so the results cannot be viewed.

Wearing shoes and outerwear that can be easily removed prior to weighing usually simplifies the process. Some medical offices prefer to weigh their patients with their shoes on, while others do not. It's best for all patients to be weighed in a consistent way, since coats, jackets and footwear can vary widely in weight from visit to visit and season to season.

One other interesting point to note is that home scales tend to weigh patients optimistically light. Either that or patients tend to remember their weight in a more favorable light compared to what was shown on their doctor's scale. One's exact weight may vary from scale to scale, but remember, it's one's change in weight that we're really monitoring. Your physician's staff should weigh you on the same scale each time a weight is needed so a reliable picture is available when assessing one's overall health.

Blood pressure is one of the most important vital signs that can be monitored and tends to be taken more often than pulse and respiratory rate. In many primary care offices, blood pressures are taken on adult patients with nearly every visit. Wearing sleeves or clothing that can be easily raised or removed to expose your upper arm is helpful when assessing a patient's blood pressure. Sometimes checking a blood pressure measurement through clothing can be done, but certain garments will not allow it. As a general rule, this is not a recommended practice. A stethoscope should be placed directly upon the skin to most accurately record one's blood pressure.

Should you be under a doctor's care for the treatment of high blood pressure, recording your readings on a regular basis for review by your physician can be helpful. Some patients become nervous in a physician's office, resulting in higher-than-average blood pressure readings. This common effect is referred to as "white coat hypertension." Also blood pressure readings can vary widely between morning and evening hours with the highest reading generally occurring between 7:00 a.m. and 9:00 a.m. This predictable change in blood pressure is referred to as a form of circadian rhythm. Circadian rhythm can be described as a predictable biologic phenomenon that occurs on regular basis during a twenty-four hour period. One's circadian rhythm is often altered by prolonged changes in work schedules, as in those who work the graveyard or overnight shift. Frequent shift changes may not allow one's circadian rhythm to adjust, accounting for symptoms resulting in decreased alertness or a decreased sense of well-being.

A representative number of blood pressure readings taken at various times of the day and in various environments can be quite helpful in the diagnosis and treatment of illnesses. Accurate, inexpensive, easy-to-use, automatic, blood pressure monitoring machines are readily available at drugstores and discount department stores. When visiting your physician for evaluation of high blood pressure, remember to bring in fifteen to twenty blood pressure readings taken at home or at work.

After the office nurse has taken your blood pressure, occasionally your pulse, respiratory rate and temperature may be checked as well. The need for these measurements will vary depending on the problems you may be experiencing.

It is commonplace to take a child's temperature when they come to their physician's office with an illness. This practice is sometimes misleading, because wide temperature swings can occur over a short span of hours. A parent may claim that their child had a recent fever of 103 degrees Fahrenheit. However, the office nurse records a temperature of 99.5 degrees. The course of many illnesses is often marked by fairly wide temperature variations from time to time. The exact temperature your child has is usually not as important as simply the fact that your child is suffering from a febrile illness; an illness associated with fever. There are certainly exceptions to this rule and your physician will know when it's appropriate to take someone's temperature.

In the same vein, it's been shown that many of the commonly used instruments to measure temperature from a patient's ear are frequently inaccurate. Some of us could make a case for going back to thermometers.

Talking with a Nurse or Your Physician:

After appropriate vital signs have been taken by the nurse, she will usually review the reasons for your visit. This is an important part of your visit and, if handled correctly, will allow your physician to more appropriately and effectively handle your problems. Most primary care physicians are capable of treating many different problems. Realizing this, patients frequently hope to address two or more problems per visit. The complexity of a problem and time requirements to analyze different problems can vary widely. Patients often do not realize that they have been scheduled for a ten- to fifteen-minute appointment. They simply believe they have been scheduled to see their doctor and whatever is required in time or services will be provided. In the real world, this may not be achievable, due to the pressures of everyday medicine unless proper provisions have been made. I can't emphasize enough, should you wish to review several problems at a single visit, request a longer-than-average appointment time at the time of scheduling.

To facilitate the process and improve your chances of success, follow a few basic ground rules during your interviewing process with a nurse or physician. First, don't confuse a symptom with a disease. Understanding the difference between a symptom and a disease will improve your understanding of how medical interviewing is conducted. A symptom is a feeling or a sign that a certain disease or physical disorder exists. For example, pain and cough are symptoms. A symptom gives your physician a clue about what may be the cause of your disease or disorder. By itself, a single symptom is usually not enough to diagnose the exact nature of your disorder. The same symptom can be a sign of many different diseases or problems. For example, chest pain can be due to heart disease, stomach disorders, pneumonia, chest wall pain, sports injuries and many other conditions. In a lifetime, patients will experience the same or very similar symptoms for several different disorders. When questioned by a health care worker, you may believe that your symptoms indicate the same problem you had experienced in the past because to you they seem identical. They may indeed be indicative of the same problem, but more often than not, your current symptoms represent a different illness.

When suffering from an acute problem such as an infectious disease, a patient will generally experience one or more symptoms. You may, for example, have a severe cough combined with a sore throat or a painfully swollen gland. Your doctor will elicit a number of symptoms from you, but your primary or most uncomfortable symptom is often the key to your illness. Make sure your physician does not lose track of which ache or pain is the most intolerable. After I have fully questioned each patient about his or her illness, I often ask, "If you could choose only one worst symptom, what would it be? Is it your cough? Is it your sore throat? Which is your primary symptom?" Secondly, do not leave your doctor's office without having your primary symptom evaluated and treated.

Sometimes a small detail can provide a critical clue to you medical problem. An interesting example comes to mind. Not too long ago a young woman came to my office with a cluster of symptoms consisting of a nonproductive cough, fever, chills, severe headache, and physical findings compatible with pneumonia. Blood tests also showed a low white blood count typical of what could be found with a viral pneumonia. The picture didn't make sense, since the young woman seemed to be sicker than I would have expected with what appeared to be a common flu like illness. After further probing I learned that my patient was suffering from a potentially life-threatening disease – psittacosis, which is caused by a tiny organism, chlamydia psittaci. Her infected pet bird was the cause of her serious illness. This organism can also be found in turkeys when infected flocks are rounded up for processing. Without knowing about her pet bird the problem may have gone undiagnosed. Many illnesses are linked to your environment. Awareness of this point may play an important role in determining the cause and thus the treatment of your illness.

Many patients attempt self-diagnosis inadvertently misleading their physician and themselves. Often, this is not intentional. They simply state from the onset of their office visit,

"Dr. Caravella, I have strep throat again," or "That darn gout is acting up again." Maybe so, maybe not.

Patients can mislead themselves and even sometimes a busy physician by self-diagnosis. Other common examples of self-diagnosis include a patient claiming to have "pneumonia," "heart pain," "sinus infection," and so on. Headaches are another very common cause of confusion for patients. In my experience, patients misdiagnose their problems over fifty percent of the time, believing they have a problem that in fact they do not have. Your physician is being paid to diagnose your problem, so let him do so.

Also, remember that a symptom rarely occurs in a vacuum; commonly it is clustered with other symptoms pointing to a specific disease. You may be experiencing other symptoms along with your headache – such as fever, cough, facial pain, sore throat, ear pain and so on. Your doctor will try to elicit all of your symptoms, and when carefully done, he may then be able to categorize them into a group of possibilities referred to as a differential diagnosis. The differential diagnosis for the above group of symptoms may include the flu, a sinus infection, strep throat, or several other possibilities. Should you have a thick, discolored drainage dripping down the back of your throat associated with the other symptoms listed, you may indeed have a sinus infection. But you may not. The important thing to remember is to describe the sensations that you are experiencing. Allowing your physician to direct the interview will provide an opportunity for him or her to search for all possible symptoms, hopefully leading to a correct diagnosis.

When possible, you should give careful thought before your office visit about your symptoms. You may even want to write your symptoms down before your visit. When speaking with a nurse, list in order of importance which symptoms are of most concern to you. All too often, patients initially mention only a single problem to the nurse. After their doctor has used up nearly the entire appointment dealing with a single problem, they then proceed to mention one or two additional problems which are sometimes more serious than their initial complaint.

124

If your physician knows all of your problems up front, he can select the ones he feels require his most urgent attention. He can pace himself accordingly and then reserve the least important complaints for future visits. This system leads to the highest degree of patient satisfaction.

Awareness of the onset of your symptoms, frequency, duration, and severity will prove to be very useful in putting together a diagnosis. In some cases, it is easy to know when a symptom first occurred. For example, if you fall on ice and break your wrist, it's obvious when your problem began. Other situations may not be as obvious. Some patients will suffer with their symptoms for weeks, months or even years before deciding to see their physician. By then, dates and memories may have become vague.

Not all is lost however. Carefully *estimating* the time frame of various symptoms can prove to be almost as effective as knowing exact dates. When your doctor asks you to estimate when your problem first began, try to avoid such answers as, "A long time ago," "A while ago," or "I can't remember." "A long time ago" to a teenager is two or three days ago. For the rest of us, it's usually months or even years ago. Be as specific as possible. For example, one could respond, "It started about two or three months ago." A good guess is clearly more helpful than a vague answer such as, "A while ago."

The next important question to be answered is whether or not your symptom is continuous or tends to come and go. Does it occur several times a day? Maybe it happens twice a week or once a month. Possibly it's always there. How long does the pain or numbness last? Does it last for seconds, minutes, hours or days? Estimates to all these questions will provide useful information to allow your physician to help you.

Most diseases or medical problems are fairly uniform in how they act. They fall into certain known patterns or categories of predictability. Providing specific details will allow your doctor to lump your problem into one or two smaller categories.

Is your symptom worse at night, in the morning, afternoon or in the evening? Many conditions are worse at certain times of the day. For example, coughing may be more prominent at night when you are suffering from pneumonia or other respiratory infections. If the cough is due to exercise-induced asthma, it will be worse with activity and is unlikely to occur at rest. Many children with exercise-induced asthma may only experience a cough and will not necessarily have shortness of breath or wheezing.

When your symptoms occur, see if they are linked to activities, rest, meals, fasting or even medication use. It helps to pay close attention to what you're doing, as well as being aware of what is happening around you, when trying to understand the cause of your symptoms. Some problems are worse at home, at work or in school. The environment may be an important issue. Air quality, dust or pollutants can affect some patients. Temperatures can make a difference. Animal exposure may be a factor. Unfortunately in some cases, no patterns related to the onset of your symptoms will be apparent.

Rest relieves some symptoms, and worsens others. What activity, if any, worsens your symptoms? Many patients develop symptoms related to new exercise programs, additional job activities or even exertion related to home remodeling projects or hobbies.

Meals can be related to many problems. Symptoms may occur during or after a meal. A variety of foods can cause a whole host of difficulties for some patients. For example patients with gall stones or gall bladder disease will often suffer from fatty food intolerance. Fried foods can cause terrible symptoms in these patients shortly after eating a meal. Other patients can develop indigestion from excess use of coffee or carbonated soft drinks. Once again, a pattern may become evident after careful thought.

Many of us lead very active as well as complicated lives. A large percentage of women work full time jobs outside of their homes, care for children, prepare meals and do more than their share of household duties. This situation can lead to high levels of stress, anxiety and often depression. Stressful situations contribute to a whole host of medical problems. Some patients under stress deny that their symptoms are related to their personal problems or to their work situation. Should your level of stress be higher at work, your symptoms may more likely occur immediately before or during your workday. Sometimes even the thought of work is enough to make many of you sick. *You know who you are.* Now you need to tell your doctor.

As you can see there exists a variety of possibilities as well as extenuating circumstances that can contribute to your health. Your doctor will help sort out these issues, however any help provided by you will shorten the search and reduce the need for extensive testing.

Keeping a diary is one of the best ways to prepare for an office visit if your problem seems to be ongoing. One of the more common diaries kept by women is that of their menstrual cycle. If you are suffering from premenstrual syndrome (PMS), a diary can help your physician sort out your problem. When recording your symptoms in your diary, provide the time of the day – along with exact dates in chronological order – to explain your symptoms. Keeping an accurate diary is one of the more reliable methods of tracking complicated problems. Patterns may be seen more readily when scanning symptoms over a timeline. Unfortunately, diaries are underused. Keep this tool in mind when you or your physician are struggling to find a probable diagnosis of your problem. Medicine is a lot like detective work. The smallest clue will often provide the exact cause.

Diaries can be particularly important when dealing with the problems of children. Good, clear facts written in chronological order can provide answers to problems that would otherwise go undiagnosed. On occasion, patients or their children will see several physicians without being correctly diagnosed. Should you be one of those difficult-to-diagnose patients, a carefully detailed diary may provide the elusive answer your doctor is searching for.

Your diary should be composed of brief sentences recording the time of day your symptoms occur and their duration. Recording meal times along with foods and beverages consumed may prove helpful. Even noting activities and exercise patterns will help if your symptoms occur more often with sports, dancing or other vigorous exercises. In your diary, record if your problems occur at home, at work or in school. Are your symptoms worse on the weekends or during the workweek? Keeping track of these types of issues will be helpful when your physician reviews your diary.

Diaries can also be useful when dealing with long-term problems of adolescents. Many adolescents experience difficulty in remembering or paying attention to the details of their illness. When they talk with physicians, their histories are often vague. Their lack of knowledge about symptoms or problems may be related to the fact that they view illness as a short-term problem not worthy of much time or effort. Most of the time they are correct and their symptoms clear up almost as quickly as they came. When they are not so fortunate, their problems may prove challenging or confusing. Sometimes, a carefully written diary will contain the necessary clues needed to sort out their difficulties.

Some adults also struggle when it comes to remembering details of their medical problems. This can be particularly true for patients with obesity problems. Adults tend to underestimate the amount of food or number of calories that they consume on a daily basis. Many overweight patients describe meals and snacks that sound quite healthy, yet they still seem to be overweight. Keeping an accurate one-week diary of all snacks and meals eaten may be informative for patients and physicians alike. Volumes, sizes or weights of each food item should be estimated as closely as possible. Only then can one determine a calorie count with some degree of accuracy.

Another example can further demonstrate this point. A gentleman standing five feet eight inches tall and weighing about 285 pounds came in to visit me one day for advice on treating his elevated blood pressure. He was of average bone and muscle mass and should have weighed approximately 160 pounds. Because high blood pressure can sometimes be caused by excessive weight, I decided to question him about his eating habits. I asked him to relate to me what he usually eats between meals and at meal times as well. For breakfast, he often ate bran cereal, a small glass of orange juice and one cup of coffee. I commended him on his choices since these foods were part of my usual diet as well. He stated he ate no snacks between breakfast and lunch. At lunch, he usually had a light bowl of soup and a small salad. Once again, I was impressed and complimented him on his choices. He also *denied* intake of afternoon snacks, dinner or even evening snacks. His activity level was average, and he lacked any thyroid or other known medical disorders that would influence his weight. I knew, therefore, that he must have been forgetting several hundred calories somewhere along the line, since a man of this size by any nutritionist's estimate would require more than this amount of food to maintain this degree of girth. This example represents a case in which a diet history was not accurate for reasons not determined.

The above case is an extreme example, since most of us are more aware of what we are doing wrong with our diets. Sometimes admitting it to ourselves is difficult. An *accurate* food diary may reveal – both to us and to our physicians – at least some of our indiscretions.

In summary, one cannot say enough about presenting good, clear facts to your physician about the history of any medical problem. If there is one thing that often gets in the way of a correct diagnosis of an illness, it is the lack of sufficient or accurate facts available to your physician during your initial office visit.

Chapter 25

The Physical Examination Can Get Physical

After a thorough history, the second most important part of every office visit is the physical examination. Physical findings from examinations are absolutely critical to determine a cause for a problem in nearly every patient encounter. We have all heard the saying, "a picture is worth a thousand words," and this is especially true in the art of physical examination. Descriptive terms, no matter how accurate, can rarely replace the actual examination. For example, a patient may call in claiming to have "poison ivy" and request to be treated over the phone. Occasionally, however, the rash has a secondary infection with bacteria such as staphylococcus, unbeknownst to the patient. If that is the case, traditional treatment could worsen the condition and allow the infection to spread.

Some of the smallest differences between diseases can only be determined by the physical examination. Bronchitis, for example, can often be distinguished from pneumonia only by listening to lung sounds with a stethoscope. The extent of the physical examination will vary significantly influenced by the specific problem your physician is attempting to address. For example, if one is visiting their doctor to have a mole checked, then simply looking at the mole or skin lesion is often sufficient. If, however, the mole is truly suspicious and there is a concern for a malignancy, your doctor may also look for an enlarged lymph node in the vicinity of the skin lesion to evaluate for possible metastatic (cancerous) spread.

If one has suffered hand trauma, there is little reason to perform an extensive examination beyond the involved extremity. If however a patient has a swollen or red-looking thumb, the diagnostic possibilities are much greater, and a more comprehensive history and physical exam may be necessary to evaluate for infectious diseases or inflammatory arthritis such as gout.

The causes of unexplained fever or weight loss can be variable, complicated, and may require a comprehensive physical examination and appropriate testing to determine the final diagnosis. Often, to fully understand how a problem alters or affects your body your physician will have to examine you completely. Shortcuts may lead to misdiagnosis.

Comprehensive physical exams should be performed for patients with several problems, a complicated problem, or those wishing to be fully evaluated on a periodic basis. Many patients fear physical examinations, or they are extremely offended or embarrassed by them. Some patients believe examinations are uncomfortable or even painful. Should you decide to avoid an examination out of fear or embarrassment, this could result in delayed or inadequate medical care. Only on rare occasions, after explaining the facts to them, have I had patients absolutely refuse an examination. A caring physician will usually be able to put your mind at ease by explaining carefully what should be done and why. Your doctor usually wants you to be well-informed and content with your choices.

It is true that some examinations are uncomfortable, but most of them are not too difficult to bear. As most people realize, there is no substitute for an appropriate, hands-on examination. An inadequate exam may result in misdiagnosis, unnecessary tests and delays in proper treatment. Missing or delaying a diagnosis eventually will result in more pain and suffering on the part of those patients who refuse to be properly examined.

During an examination, it may be tempting to ask questions before the process is completed. "How is it, Doc?" is a common question. "How is my heart?" Of course, most of us are anxious about what our doctors have found – good, bad or otherwise. It is in one's best interest, however, to wait until the exam has been completed before reviewing the outcome. Your physician will often not have a clear picture until the entire process has been finished. Once done, he will be able to piece together the historical facts presented earlier with all of your physical findings; thereby, coming up with a list of diagnostic possibilities. At this time, laboratory tests may or may not be necessary to reduce the problem to a single diagnosis. Once your physician has a working diagnosis he will be able to proceed with effective treatment.

When symptomatic relief is urgent, an experienced practitioner will be able to provide comfort or help even when a firm diagnosis has not been established by testing. All would agree that pain and suffering must be attended to as early as possible.

Even though your physician may have a reasonable idea of what ails you, it may not be sufficient to warrant the use of expensive or even potentially harmful medications, surgical procedures or treatment plans without first pinpointing or confirming his thoughts. Therefore, long-term benefits or cures in many instances will require going the extra mile in the form of limited or extensive testing. The amount of testing performed varies from specialty to specialty. Family practitioners tend to feel comfortable with less testing than general internists or specialists having over the years developed a different working image of diseases and feel less of a compulsion to perform extensive tests.

Chapter 26

Laboratory Testing: An Evolving Art

"Doc, can you run a few tests and check me out?" This is a common request heard nearly daily in most primary care offices everywhere. Patients erroneously believe that laboratory tests, x-rays and other forms of testing are the most important part of any medical evaluation. In fact, x-rays and lab studies are often less important than patients realize. After a thorough history and physical examination, lab tests should confirm what an experienced physician already suspects. Most of the tests physicians request are usually very helpful. In fact, they are indispensable. Patients, however, tend to put too much faith in testing and do not pay enough homage to the other methods of evaluation I have covered.

There are literally thousands of possible blood tests, urine tests, stool studies, x-rays and other studies available for physicians to choose from. Every bodily fluid can be examined and evaluated, whether it be joint fluid, blood specimens or vaginal secretions. The possibilities are limitless, and there is no *short list* of tests that can be done, as patients often request, to provide all of the answers that patients hope to hear. When possible, the best course to follow is to perform the fewest tests that will give the most accurate answers.

Selecting the right test can be very difficult – especially when a diagnosis is uncertain or difficult to categorize. For example, there are many causes of chronic pain in clinically ill patients. Pain can be due to countless disorders requiring extensive use of scans and blood tests for correct diagnosis. Selecting the appropriate tests to perform within the constraints of managed care remains difficult at times but is usually doable.

In the field of primary care, many symptoms that patients develop may have their roots in one of several causes. Some patients falsely believe that a quick visit to their physician will resolve their questions. This is too often not the case. Fortunately however, with most initial visits a patient's worst

135

fears can generally be alleviated even without having test results immediately at hand.

As most patients realize, in the early stages of some conditions, only specific tests will offer an accurate diagnosis. A good example of this is represented by the total cholesterol blood test.   Sure, there are known cases of patients with high cholesterol levels based purely on history or physical examination. But these are unusual situations. Blood testing is the only way to evaluate a patient's cholesterol level before more dramatic symptoms or physical findings caused by this problem becomes apparent.

Probably one of the most common examples of using clinical judgment rather than testing in everyday medical practice concerns the management of common respiratory tract infections.   Many respiratory infections exhibit similar symptoms and characteristics. It is often not possible in an office visit to determine the exact organism causing your infection. Accurate diagnostic tests for viruses and atypical organisms, though available, are often reserved for research purposes, since results may take days or weeks to obtain. Given the urgency of a problem, your physician will select – based on experience and knowledge – what he or she believes to be the best treatment for your illness without necessarily the need to utilize testing.

In the past, some physicians were over-zealous, often spending large amounts of money on unnecessary tests. The current medical climate discourages testing that cannot be substantiated by facts. Many insurance companies now require a diagnostic code to accompany a test, or they will deny coverage. This policy sometimes leads to denial of preventive treatment or x-rays because they are not cost effective – meaning that not enough people have suffered or died from certain diseases to warrant the cost of "routine" testing as a screening procedure.

Some screening procedures such as mammography and prostate exams with PSA (prostatic specific antigen) blood levels have been accepted by mainstream medical science as a way to detect early cancer, but they are not necessarily covered by all insurance companies. In many states such as Ohio, women's

136

efforts through legislative means have paid off with mammography as it is a covered expense by most health plans. In contrast, the same is not true for PSA blood tests to detect early prostate cancer unless you are age 65 or over. For example, should you have an enlarged prostate gland without any nodules or clinical evidence of cancer, measuring your prostatic specific antigen (PSA) level to detect early cancer will not be a covered expense. Should you eventually develop an elevated PSA level, then the blood test becomes a covered expense as a means of tracking your status. As a result of these policies, patients sometimes refuse to pay for screening procedures until it is too late. Once the existence of a disease has been established, your physician through the use of specific diagnostic codes is given a free hand in the management and treatment of your problem. Until then, you may be on your own to search for potential health problems, including those that may occur in first-degree relatives such as parents and siblings. Simply fearing that you may harbor a serious disease fails to be an adequate reason for most insurance companies to cover a screening test.

Let's say that you wish to know what your cholesterol level is since you have never previously had it checked. Some insurance companies may pay for the initial cholesterol level, but not always. Should you decide to pay for the test to establish a baseline, and it's found to be abnormal, then future tests obtained at specific intervals will be a covered expense. This also assumes that your doctor uses the correct diagnostic code for billing purposes once you are found to have high cholesterol. Some patients **known** to have high cholesterol levels wish to have their tests repeated more often than considered medically necessary to relieve their fears. Insurance plans often do not cover too-frequent testing, and you may be billed accordingly.

There is some good news, however. Some insurance companies promote specific tests to detect diseases in their earliest stages. In fact, many insurance companies conduct chart audits or chart inspections to make sure physicians are performing approved screening tests. Insurance companies differ on what they consider to be worthwhile screening tests.

Published guidelines are available, however, and **many recommendations appear in the appendix. You must become intimately familiar with these guidelines and use them to the best of your ability.**

Guidelines for routine or preventive medicine studies are usually determined by Medicare, and then other health insurers follow suit. Major health organizations, such as the American Cancer Society, the American Medical Association, the American Academy of Family Practice and numerous other influential organizations and agencies present their recommendations based on current research, and when enough agreement is reached, policies are instituted. After consideration by physician-quality-control panels working with the insurance industry, many recommendations are accepted for reimbursement. One must check their insurance manual to determine if their test is a covered expense. It may be prudent to pay for recommended tests should they not be reimbursable.

Cervical Cancer Screening:

One of the best known recommendations is the Papanicolaou (PAP) test. Cancer of the cervix is the seventh most common cancer. It is generally caused by the sexually transmitted human papilloma virus (HPV) and it is a cancer that rarely if ever occurs in virgins. The PAP smear has resulted in a 50% reduction in death from cervical cancer. As good as the PAP smear is, it has been improved upon and has now been replaced by the "thin prep" cytologic (cellular) study. The speciman for the "thin prep" is obtained in the same fashion as the PAP test. Instead of the cervical speciman being placed on a slide where only a few cells will attach for future viewing, the cervical fluid and cells are placed in a special bath where over 90% of the cells are available for evaluation. This new technique provides a much larger selection of cells for analysis. According to Dr. Jerome Belinson, Chairman of the Department of Obstetrics and Gynecology at The Cleveland Clinic Foundation, "the new test under study since 1997, has substantially improved the detection rate of both early and late stage cervical cancers," while dramatically reducing the number of uncertain (atypical cells) or questionable PAP tests that have been in the past, difficult to classify. The Agency for Health Care Policy and Research associated with Duke University has reviewed over 900 articles concerning cervical cancer screening tests at one, two and three year intervals. This research concluded that when the "thin prep" is employed for cervical cancer screening, it results in earlier and more accurate cancer detection. The ultimate benefits of using the "thin prep" test over the PAP test has resulted in fewer hysterectomies, lower rates of chemotherapy, lower rates of radiation therapy and an over all lower death rate from cervical cancer. This new test will also detect, if requested by you or your physician, the following STD's (sexually transmitted diseases); chlamydia (chlamydia trachomatis), gonorrhea (neisseria gonorrhea) and HPV, all from a single specimen. Wow!

Prostate Cancer screening:

Too little testing, on the other hand, can be foolhardy as well. For example, every man fifty years of age and older must consider having an annual prostate exam and PSA blood test to detect early prostate cancer. The rectal exam performed by a physician attempts to detect abnormal nodules that may exist within a man's prostate gland. By itself, the rectal exam is not sufficient and thus should be accompanied by the PSA test. Elevated PSA levels most commonly occur from benign enlargement of the prostate gland associated with aging. It's very important to remember that should an elevated PSA level be detected, another blood test known as a **Free** PSA level should then be performed. Should your physician fail to suggest it, I would recommend that you request it. If the Free PSA level is less than 11% it is suggestive of cancer. Should the Free PSA level be over 23% it is suggestive of benign disease (specific "normal" levels may vary slightly from lab to lab). A prostate gland biopsy is usually required to distinguish benign from cancerous changes. Prostate cancer, like most other cancers caught early enough, is curable.

139

Breast Cancer Evaluation:

Likewise, every woman aged forty and over requires an annual mammogram to detect early evidence of breast cancer. Some physicians recommend mammograms every two years in the forties however there is a tendency to change that recommendation to an annual test. Most physicians also recommend a base line mammogram at age 35 years. Many women avoid mammograms either out of fear of what may be found or due to the significant discomfort caused by sufficient compression of the breast tissue to allow for adequate x-ray penetration. Without adequate compression, the test lacks validity. Should a suspicious area be found within the breast by using mammography, another test known as breast ultrasound can be used to provide additional information. This is a painless technique in which sound waves are passed through breast tissue looking for changes in breast tissue density. If a suspicious area is found in the breast, one can use ultrasound to determine if it is a solid or cystic (fluid filled) mass. Partially solid or completely solid masses will require a breast biopsy. Completely fluid filled cysts are benign and do not require biopsy. Fortunately most breast tumors are benign. Ultrasound testing without mammography is not an adequate method of evaluating a patient for breast cancer.

A new form of technology believed to be superior to mammography, which will not require breast compression, will eventually replace mammography. This technology is not currently available. Women will still have to endure life saving mammography for the time being.

Frequently Requested Tests:

A number of commonly requested tests are more often than not unnecessary in the office setting under many circumstances. Both the chest x-ray and the EKG or electrocardiogram come to mind. If a patient has never smoked and has no respiratory symptoms such as cough, shortness of breath, unexplained weight loss and so on, then a chest x-ray would rarely show significant abnormal findings. About the age of forty, some physicians may suggest a baseline study that may prove to be helpful as a reference point should problems occur later in life. The problem is that a baseline study is often not covered by health insurance.

According to James F. Guitierrez, MD, Director of Regional Medical Practice Quality Control for The Cleveland Clinic Foundation, electrocardiograms and exercise stress testing in a totally normal and asymptomatic patient is also of little value. If there is a family history of hypertension (high blood pressure), diabetes, or heart attacks at a young age, then a case could be made to obtain a baseline EKG study. If a patient has led a sedentary life style and has other important risk factors as determined by their physician then an exercise stress test may prove worthwhile before beginning a strenuous exercise program. EKGs and exercise stress tests of various types are most valuable in the evaluation of patients with a known history of coronary artery disease or unexplained chest pain.

On another note, one test frequently requested by patients is their blood type. It is rarely necessary to know this information outside of the field of obstetrics. One's blood type is usually only important to know when one requires a blood transfusion for some reason, occasionally in the case of paternity testing or under other rare circumstances beyond the scope of this book. Blood typing is always conducted before a unit of blood is administered. Even when you know what your blood type is, it is still necessary to confirm your belief through repeat testing. Giving the wrong form of blood to an individual could be lethal within a matter of minutes. Confirmation of one's blood type is conducted before a transfusion. There are no exceptions to this policy.

Should you wish to know your blood type anyway, simply donating a unit of blood to your local Red Cross station will provide the information you want, free of charge. Currently, each donated unit of blood is typed and screened for AIDS, hepatitis B, hepatitis C, and any additional tests the Red Cross feels is necessary to protect its benefactors. Please remember,

there is no risk of contacting an infectious disease when one donates blood to the Red Cross. Only new, sterile equipment and techniques are used on each and every donor.

Many factors come into play when determining which tests to perform. Most often, a decision is based on your physician's judgment, knowledge, and past experience. Sometimes it is based on tried and proven recommendations. Lastly, testing is influenced by whether or not you are convinced that test results will be worth the effort and possible costs. It is also appropriate for you as a consumer and as a patient to question whether or not a test is really worthwhile. If your doctor cannot make a sound case for the performance of a specific test, the test may not be necessary.

After a test has been completed, follow up with your physician to learn the outcome. Doing a test and not knowing the results is equal to not having done the test at all. No news may not mean good news. The test specimen could have been lost. The lab slip or x-ray report may have been erroneously placed in someone else's chart. A more frequent error involves placing test results in the medical record unbeknownst to the physician and without his review. If your physician hasn't seen the test results, he will not notify you of information he also lacks. If you do not receive a phone call or written notification of your test results, be sure to inquire about them. These types of errors are fairly common and can have devastating consequences.

When considering specialized testing or risk associated procedures one must keep in mind Peter F. Drucker's statement, "There is the risk you cannot afford to take, and there is the risk you cannot afford not to take". After discussing with your PCP or specialist which tests may be needed and their associated risks, a prudent patient must then decide which course of action is best to follow. We will all face difficult decisions but they are decisions we will have to regularly decide as we continue to age. As someone once said, "getting old is only for the brave".

142

Chapter 27

Defensive Medicine

Many of you have heard the term "defensive medicine." This is the practice of ordering tests or studies of questionable importance in order to strengthen a physician's medical position in the case of a potential lawsuit. In today's medical climate, all physicians are engaged to some extent in this activity, even when they are fairly certain of the diagnosis or long-term outcomes. Sometimes defensive medicine is warranted, and sometimes it is not. The fear of cancer and its consequences is a prime example of where defensive medicine may be practiced. The problem of breast cancer being one of the most noteworthy medical problems involving woman today comes to mind. Due to the extreme fear breast cancer conjures up, mammography and other tests are used aggressively and sometimes excessively. The slightest shadow, borderline calcification, or any other departure from the norm will lead to additional mammography views, frequent follow-up breast exams, breast aspirations or biopsies, ultrasound studies and so on. For some women this process is nerve-wracking. Very few tests are more anxiety-provoking for patients and physicians than mammography and its interpretation. The science of mammography remains primitive considering the number of non-cancerous breast biopsies performed annually. Future computerized analysis of mammograms may provide some relief – not only by reducing errors of interpretation but also by reducing the number of repeated tests that may have to be performed. Newer technologies that are better tolerated are on the horizen to replace mammography.

In the final analysis, when tests are ordered, ask your doctor to explain the exact need for each test. Will the test explain something we do not understand? Is it only done for peace of mind? This may be a valid reason for a test. However, a specific diagnostic code describing your symptom or medical finding must be assigned to each test or most insurance companies will not cover its cost. We are all deserving of the best that medicine has to offer, but unnecessary tests contribute nothing to the final outcome.

Some patients, realizing they may have to pay for a non-covered test, may still wish to have the test performed to relieve their anxieties. If the test is low in risk and you are willing to accept the financial obligation, then I see no reason why the test should not be performed. You are the one who will ultimately make most decisions about medical testing. Solid education, along with confidence in your physician's abilities, will help you choose the best course to follow.

Chapter 28

Office Visit Conclusion

Dr. Clarence H. Braddock, assistant professor of medicine at the University of Washington is the lead author of a study in1993 involving 59 primary care physicians and 65 surgeons in the fields of orthopedics and general surgery. He found that the necessary criteria for informed decision making was met in only 9% of patient-physician encounters. Thus, in only a small percentage of encounters were patients adequately informed enough to understand their treatment options. He noted in his study that **no** patients were fully informed about the use of new medications. He also found that only one patient was completely informed about prostate cancer screening. Maysel Kemp White, Ph.D., associate director for the Bayer Institute for Health Care Communication in West Haven, Connecticut, which sponsored Dr. Braddock's study, commented, "If patients know what's happening, they're much more likely to follow through; and if they're involved in decision-making, they're much more likely to follow through."

According to an *American Medical News* article published January 17, 2000, Rudolph M. Navari, MD.,director of the Walther Cancer Research Center at the University of Notre Dame, claims, "There's still enormous room for improvement." His current research now focuses on how patients and their families can be taught to ask the right questions about their diagnosis.

In a recent article published in the *Journal of the American Medical Association* (JAMA) in December, 1999, Dr. Braddock refers to seven key elements that should be considered during the decision-making process. The elements listed are not an exact duplicate of his work. I have chosen to rewrite them to simplify their meaning for patients since the original work was written for physician consumption. Every attempt was made to convey Dr. Braddock's exact meaning and I hope nothing was lost in the translation.

145

(Neither JAMA nor Dr. Braddock are responsible for any variation in the interpretation from the original meaning of the seven key elements listed below.)

1. The physician should discuss with the patient, the patient's role in the process of decision-making.
2. The doctor needs to adequately discuss the medical problem with the patient. As an alternative, the doctor may need to discuss the nature of the decision the patient must make.
3. A patient may be given alternative choices and the opportunity to discuss them.
4. Discussion of the risks and benefits of a given choice may be necessary.
5. The outcome of a patient choice may not be completely predictable and thus consequences may have to be reviewed as well.
6. The physician may have to determine if their patient accurately understands his/her choices.
7. Exploring the choice that a patient prefers is required.

Under many circumstances not all of the above elements must be met. For example, if a patient has a positive throat culture for strep (meaning they have strep throat), the medical consensus is clear. The consensus is that all such patients would require treatment to prevent adverse consequences of untreated strep throat. The issue in this case is not complex as far as the need to provide treatment is concerned. Nearly all physicians would recommend treatment. Therefore the decision-making process for the patient in this case would concern what form of treatment the patient would prefer rather than whether or not to treat it. The patient would be asked to decide between either a penicillin injection or an antibiotic taken by mouth to treat their strep throat. The patient is always in charge of their own case. It may not be prudent but he/she can refuse to accept treatment and then live or die with the consequences. This scenario again assumes that the patient has been adequately informed about his

146

medical problem based on the above elements of decision making.

In the case of treating a potentially terminal illness such as cancer, the problem is vastly more complex and all elements of decision-making must be fully addressed with each patient by their physician.

As one can see, upon conclusion of your office visit, it is important that you have a comfortable working knowledge of your medical problems and overall health status. Before leaving, make sure to review in your mind why you went to visit your physician, what was said, what prescriptions were given to you, what tests were suggested, and what specialists were recommended. Not infrequently, your physician reviewed several problems and offered several suggestions. Taking brief notes during your medical visit as a refresher to be reviewed at the conclusion of your visit or at home can prove useful.

Do not leave your physician's office without knowing his or her thoughts. Usually your physician has a fairly clear idea of your problems, but he or she does not always adequately convey the message to you. Should you not understand your illness, you must alert your doctor accordingly so he or she can further explain it to you. Any condition, no matter how complex, can be explained in layman's terms. Sure, it may take time and your physician may appear rushed, but you must have a working knowledge of your problems. Patients who understand their medical problems are much more likely to fill prescriptions, take medication appropriately, complete tests that have been scheduled and return for follow-up visits.

Let's look at common problems treated daily in primary care offices across America. Being properly informed, as you will see, will encourage you to follow your physician's instructions. One of the most common chronic disorders treated by physicians is high blood pressure or hypertension. Research has shown that even mild but persistent elevations of blood pressure are quite damaging over time. Untreated or inadequately treated hypertension is one of the leading causes of kidney failure; often resulting in kidney dialysis and later kidney transplantation. Hypertension, improperly treated, is also a

147

common cause of overworking the heart, leading to a weakening of the heart muscle and eventually heart failure. High blood pressure exerts excessive force against the walls of large blood vessels, leading to hardening of the arteries. This condition causes the walls of the arteries to thicken, calcify and eventually weaken. When your blood vessels can no longer compensate for the high blood pressure, they may eventually block up or bleed within the brain, resulting in a stroke.

As you can see, any one of these three common conditions is worth preventing. Many patients are unaware of the connection between high blood pressure and its three serious consequences: stroke, kidney failure and heart failure. When patients clearly understand what they must do to remain healthy, they will rarely miss medications or follow-up office visits. Should your illness be mysterious to you, ask your physician for a clear explanation of it so that over time, you will feel comfortable with what is being done to help you. Most doctors in today's medical climate will be receptive to your ideas and needs if you present them in a useful and non-threatening way. Well intentioned physicians wish to please their patients while still providing good medical care.

The American Board of Internal Medicine has developed a patient satisfaction scale that indicates how you can assess your physician's performance after an office visit.

The American Board of Internal Medicine's Patient Satisfaction Scale

How would you rate the physician in terms of:

> Telling you everything, being truthful, upfront and frank; not keeping things from you that you should know?
>
> Greeting you warmly; calling you by the name you prefer; being friendly, never crabby or rude?
>
> Treating you like you're on the same level; never "talking down" to you or treating you like a child?

148

Letting you tell your story, listening carefully, asking
thoughtful questions, not interrupting you while
you're talking?

Showing interest in you as a person; not acting bored or
ignoring what you have to say?

Telling you during the physical exam about what he/she
is going to do and why; telling you what he/she
finds?

Discussing choices with you; asking your opinion;
offering choices and letting you decide what to
do; asking what you think before telling you
what to do?

Encouraging you to ask questions; answering them
clearly; never avoiding your questions or
lecturing you?

Explaining what you need to know about your problems,
how and why they occurred , and what to expect
next?

Using words that you can understand when explaining
your problems and treatment; explaining any
technical medical terms in plain language?

After reviewing the above scale you can rate your physician
on a scale from 1 to 5 where 1 indicates that you strongly
disagree and 5 means that you strongly agree. Should you
believe, after applying the above standards to your physician's
care that there is room for improvement, openly discuss these
matters with him or her. When given an opportunity, most
professionals are open-minded.

In summary, being well informed through discussions with
your physician is critical to the patient-physician relationship.
Good information is one of our best weapons against fear. Fear
is the child of ignorance and tends to suffocate us often robbing
us of a fighting chance. Along with understanding we need to
know our options. With knowledge and choices we can manage
or beat most illnesses rather than become enslaved or ravaged by
them. Just as importantly, you must have significant control
over your destiny. Do not leave it solely in the hands of your

physician. Doing so will increase the chances of error and omissions. Work as a team. By doing so you will achieve the highest degree of patient satisfaction and the best outcomes. You owe it to yourself and to your family to participate as fully as possible in all aspects of your health care.

Chapter 29

Telephone Medicine and "Curbstone Consultations"

The complexities of modern medicine generally tend to discourage the use of a telephone to diagnose and treat medical problems. On a daily basis, patients call medical offices, hoping to have problems diagnosed or managed over the telephone. Sometimes this is possible, but more often than not, good results cannot be achieved in this manner. Telephone management of patients' problems, though appearing inexpensive, expedient and convenient, is also likely to be fraught with error.

Another practice to be avoided is party or backyard medicine, referred to in the profession as a "curbstone consultation." Asking a physician to effectively diagnose and offer sound advice about important medical issues at an afternoon picnic is pushing the envelope of good judgment. You would be best served by calling your physician's office instead for a routine office visit. Doctors, though sometimes complimented by being given an opportunity to demonstrate their professional prowess at a social event, rarely have adequate facts at hand to make a worthwhile assessment. Please don't tempt a physician to give advice that may be tainted by lack of knowledge and the absence of a physical exam. In the end, you will be the one to suffer from this compromised form of medical care.

Chapter 30

Emergency Room Visits

Managed care insurance companies have recognized the broad services that family practitioners and other primary care physicians can provide. They can economically and efficiently treat both acute and urgent needs, and only the most serious emergencies need be directed to emergency rooms. Usually only after-hour urgent problems must be treated in emergency rooms or urgent care centers. In the past, self-directed patients would make their own decisions about where to go for help. Of course, this also led to the overuse of emergency rooms. Some patients would wait until after-hours to frequent an urgent care center or an emergency room, rather than visit their physician during routine work hours. HMOs have discouraged this practice by not reimbursing patients for unnecessary emergency room visits. Primary care practices have started to address this problem by providing evening and Saturday hours. Emergency room patrons are learning, as well, that emergency rooms are not without problems – chief among them long waits.

Emergency rooms function differently from medical offices. Emergency room physicians rarely know their patients firsthand. They are not familiar with the reliability of patients in filling prescriptions, taking medications, or returning for follow-up care. Since they are less familiar with their clientele, emergency room doctors feel a need for more information before treating and often run lab tests and x-rays while patients are waiting. After having all necessary facts in hand, they can then finally diagnose and treat their patients.

In contrast, your family doctor will provide treatment immediately, scheduling most tests for a later date. As you can see, under most circumstances visiting your family doctor is often quicker and less expensive than other alternatives.

It is important for new managed care members to realize that they must check with their primary care physicians before going to an emergency room or urgent care center. If one does not seek advanced permission to go to such a facility, your visit may not be covered by medical insurance. Such visits are rarely reimbursable after the fact. Patients frequently contact their physician *after* being seen in the emergency room, only to learn that they must pay for the emergency room costs on their own.

Of course, life- or limb-threatening emergencies do not require a confirmatory call. The most common example of a potentially life-threatening problem is unexplained chest pain. If one is experiencing a serious life- or limb-threatening problem, it is best to proceed to the nearest emergency room.

Chapter 31

Appointment Cancellations: Giving Someone a Break

"What is right is often forgotten by what is convenient."
Bodie Thoene,
Warsaw Requiem

There are many legitimate reasons why patients may be unable to keep a scheduled appointment. Patients who fail to keep or who cancel appointments at the last minute are referred to as "no shows" in medical offices. Missed appointments that have been appropriately canceled and rescheduled do not cause problems for most physicians' practices. In busy practices, canceled appointments with as little as two hours' notice can often be successfully filled, thereby helping other needy patients arrange for a last minute appointment. In contrast, unfilled appointment slots are lost forever, resulting in sick patients going to emergency rooms or urgent care centers rather than seeing their own physician. In canceling your appointment, you may be helping other people in need.

Chapter 32

The Follow-Up Office Visit

Often it is important to return to visit your physician for a follow-up office visit to monitor your status or ongoing recovery. This is especially important with serious infections such as pneumonia, skin infections and dozens of other diseases and problems. How well patients do with treatment programs varies widely. Follow-up visits can be crucial in adjusting therapy to obtain optimum results. It is surprising how often patients leave their physician's office without scheduling a follow up office appointment even when they are asked to do so. It is just as remarkable how often patients fail to return for follow up visits after being placed on a new medication that could have unexpected results. There are no two humans exactly alike and thus outcomes are not predictable nor guaranteed. In the eyes of a physician, the management of **every** patient is an experiment. Your physician will conduct a trial with one of many possible medications when searching for a cure or control of a disease. He or she will need to see you on follow-up visits to monitor your progress or lack there of as the case may be. Medicine is an art form and not a pure science. It is not uncommon to start out with a short one to three week course of treatment to see if satisfactory results will result and then proceed accordingly.

The same holds true for many conditions. A very common example involves the management of high blood pressure. There is no guarantee a particular medication or a certain dosage will work according to plan. The management of most medical problems, I'm afraid to say, is based on trial and error. That is why we call it the practice of medicine. We try something and if it works, we're all very grateful. If it doesn't, we give something else a try. In summary, a follow-up appointment is often a necessity. Failure to return for further evaluation after your initial visit may result in dire consequences.

Disappointing Medical Care

Let's not forget the occasional situation where you felt unimpressed by the doctor or his office staff. When this happens, some patients simply give up. However, failure to follow through with a scheduled appointment may result in unfavorable outcomes over time. If this happens, make sure you schedule another appointment with a new physician as soon as possible. Most common problems such as high blood pressure, diabetes, high cholesterol, and arthritis do not go away as much as we would like them to. Do not turn a bad situation into a worse one. As a partner in your health care, you have an obligation to provide the best possible care for yourself, even when your original plans have failed. Sometimes you must be your own advocate in obtaining the best possible medical care for yourself and your family.

SECTION IV: MEDICATIONS

Chapter 33

Medications: "Thank goodness there is medicine to help me."

Many of you have an aversion to the use of new drugs or medications. Frequently, after a patient has been carefully evaluated and counseled for a chronic problem, medications may be recommended. Patients often reply, "I would prefer a natural way of controlling the problem." The implication of this comment, of course, is the possibility that some other method such as weight loss, exercise, dietary changes, relaxation techniques or other non-medical approaches may solve their problems. In some cases, these methods can work, and a three-month trial may be useful and recommended.

Sometimes patients fail to achieve their goals, either because of insufficient effort or problems beyond their control. Genetics, for instance, can interfere with our best efforts. When this is the case, eating a proper diet, regular exercise and similar practices in conjunction with medications are often recommended. Some patients who lose weight, exercise regularly and eat properly may be able to stop their medications, but unfortunately many will have to continue their medications indefinitely. Achieving and maintaining a normal weight will solve many problems for patients. Stopping medication even when this has been achieved, however, must happen only after consultation with your physician. Not all problems are solved by weight control and exercise; normal weight and active patients may still require medication to control their blood pressure, cholesterol, and other problems such as diabetes.

Occasionally, when being placed on medication, a patient will respond by saying, "I was afraid of that." In contrast, we should try to think differently, remarking instead, "Thank goodness there is medicine to help me."

To other patients a more "natural way" implies the use of herbs or other naturally-occurring substances. Many of these products have fostered huge followings, since people remain health conscious and because the natural way appeals to us as being safe and readily available to the general public. Natural substances or remedies can be used on our own and at our own convenience. Unfortunately, most of these remedies have little if any medicinal value. Yes, they may have active ingredients, but possibly only trace amounts that would generally have little biologic effects. They often have impressive and descriptive names, but they rarely perform in scientific studies as claimed. Since the ingredients are fairly inert in most of these "natural substances," the Federal Drug Administration does not require testing before sales are permitted. A lot of money is spent on these products, while often achieving only limited results. If you choose to try this approach to manage your medical problems, it may be best done under the guidance of your physician who can monitor the results and advise you accordingly.

Other patients may say, "I'm afraid of medication." Here they are referring to dangerous side effects they have read or heard about. What these patients often don't think about is that their disease is usually much more dangerous than the **likely** side effects of a prescription medication. Once your physician has recommended a medication to use, he has already decided that the benefits of using that medication substantially outweigh the risks or he would not have prescribed the medication in the first place.

Our goals are always to help rather than to do harm. Not treating a dangerous health problem guarantees serious consequences. On the other hand, medications can be carefully monitored through follow-up visits and specialized testing. Running changes can be made at any time to achieve optimum results with little real risk to patients. In some situations, such as extremely high blood pressure, no time should be wasted; medication must be started immediately.

In some cases your physician may be willing to experiment with more conservative methods such as: low salt diets, salt substitutes, dietary changes, exercise patterns or other remedies. The seriousness of the problem will determine the best course of action. In many instances however medications are more effective than other methods of treatment and should be started early in the management of many conditions.

Most likely, your use of prescription medications will increase as you get older. As we age, our biological systems are slowly failing. Research has shown that normal kidney function by the age of forty diminishes thereafter by ten percent per decade, as measured by blood and urine testing. Therefore a normal 60 year old would have kidney function 20-30% less than a younger individual. As time goes on, each of our systems are slowly deteriorating, and health problems are inevitable. Protective estrogen levels in women, for instance, begin to fail in middle age – signaling the onset of menopause. Many medications prescribed today are required simply to maintain the status quo. As we age, cholesterol levels and blood pressure levels tend to climb. Good health requires good control of these problems. Left unchecked, other systems will begin to fail. Heart failure and strokes are often the result of inadequate medication usage.

Due to busy schedules or various bad habits, some patients prefer to take pills in the morning, while others prefer evening or bedtime use. If you have a preference, some medications can be tailored to adjust to your schedule, so please discuss options with your physician. The more convenient it is to take your medications, the more likely it is that you will do so.

Chapter 34

Allergic Drug Reactions vs. Adverse Side Effects

Many patients are allergic to one or more medications. An allergic reaction is one in which your body develops antibodies to a foreign substance and reacts with the sudden onset of hives, a generalized rash, severe respiratory distress or a dangerous drop in blood pressure. Sometimes, however, appearances can be deceiving. In other words, patients sometimes claim that they have experienced an allergic reaction when in fact, after evaluation, it turned out they were simply experiencing a side effect. Many patients have been told, for example, that they were allergic to penicillin, but skin tests fail to confirm their claims. Many of these mistakes occur because patients will often phone their doctor about "hives" or rashes but are never asked to come in for examination. As a result the patient will often misdiagnose what actually has occurred. They then are labeled as being allergic to some substance when in fact they are not. Proper medical evaluation of any adverse drug reaction cannot be over emphasized.

It is common for patients to confuse side effects with allergies, but side effects and allergic reactions are two entirely different things. Side effects, though often annoying and potentially serious, do not preclude the future use of a suspicious medication or the use of a closely-related drug. Side effects may include any number of reactions that usually are annoying and even dangerous, but generally not lethal. An example of a side effect often experienced by patients is an upset stomach from the use of aspirin or codeine. In some patients, small amounts of blood loss from the stomach can occur from the repeated use of aspirin. Over time, anemia or a low blood count may result. Even severe bleeding from the stomach may occur, as indicated by the passing of black stool.

On the other hand, codeine tends to cause an upset stomach and vomiting in sensitive patients, but rarely bleeding. Taking medication with food will often reduce or eliminate an upset stomach, though not all medications can be taken with food because their effects may be reduced or eliminated. Another common side effect from the use of codeine is tiredness or sedation, which is actually sometimes an advantage when ill. The examples mentioned above all represent side effects and not allergic reactions.

Since they can be potentially lethal, drug allergies must be taken more seriously than side effects. A patient's allergy to a drug precludes any use of that drug and sometimes any closely-related drugs. For example, if someone is allergic to penicillin, they will also be allergic to ampicillin and amoxicillin, both of which are in the penicillin family of antibiotics.

In contrast, not all drugs in a family of drugs have the same side effects. In a given family of medications, some drugs may upset one's stomach while others may not. Some may cause headaches while others will not. Side effects are more easily dealt with and may even diminish with repeated use or by varying how and when a medicine is taken. If a drug routinely causes drowsiness or lightheadedness, it may be taken at bedtime; in this fashion, one can even use the side effect as an advantage. The side effects of some medications can also be reduced when they are taken with food.

Some patients avoid all use of a medication because of an initial experience with side effects. Future use of many offending medications, however, remains possible if you discuss the problems with your doctor; most physicians can help you manage unwanted side effects.

Some side effects are quite obvious, such as an upset stomach occurring fifteen to thirty minutes after taking a medication. On other occasions the possible link to a medication is much more subtle or elusive. ACE inhibitors are medications frequently used to treat high blood pressure. They can also cause a side effect easily overlooked as being linked, even by experienced physicians. Ten to fifteen percent of patients who take ACE inhibitors will experience a persistent, low-grade, dry cough. The cough may not start immediately, but rather days, weeks or even months after being on the medication. Thus, the

166

connection between a symptom and a medication may not be apparent.

In the past, physicians often overlooked the ACE connection when evaluating patients with a cough. When ACE inhibitors were first used to treat blood pressure problems, a cough was not commonly recognized as being linked to their use. Many physicians performed complicated medical evaluations on these patients to sort out the cause of their unexplained cough, finally discovering that their patients' blood pressure medication was the culprit. In these cases, stopping their blood pressure medicine resulted in the disappearance of their cough within a few weeks.

Even though most medications are capable of causing annoying side effects, only a small percentage of patients need to discontinue a medication due to complications or side effects. Most importantly, you should never stop using a prescription medication without first consulting your physician.

There are two important points worth repeating. First, unusual symptoms that cannot be explained are sometimes due to one of your medications. Knowing this point however, you should never stop a medication without first calling your physician. You may, however, delay taking your next dose. In the meantime, contact your doctor and ask if your medication could be a possible cause of your symptoms. He or she will be able to advise you about the best course of action. Secondly, any suspected adverse drug reactions or allergic reactions must be reported to your physician so that proper guidance can be provided for your future benefit.

Chapter 35

The Pharmacy Visit

Going to a reputable, full-service pharmacy is an important part of everyone's health care. There are several issues that you must consider before your trip to the pharmacy. First and foremost, investigate whether or not your health insurance carrier requires that you go to specific pharmacies or chains to ensure reimbursement. This is frequently the case because contracts have been negotiated between pharmacies and insurers to provide for special pricing. Going to an unlisted pharmacy may prevent reimbursement or result in lower levels of coverage for patients using prescription medications. Modern medications are becoming very expensive, frequently exceeding the cost of your physician's office visit. Therefore, proper care in the purchase of medications is warranted.

Many pharmaceutical chains maintain computerized records that reduce errors in filling prescriptions. This approach also simplifies refilling medications when the time comes. In fact, some large national chains are capable of refilling prescriptions for out-of-state travelers who originally acquired the prescription medication in their home state. Remember, always carry your medications in their original containers when traveling, especially controlled substances such as narcotics or sedatives. This practice is especially important when crossing international borders, where you might be stopped and searched.

Another worthwhile practice is going to the same pharmacy on a regular basis so that you will become acquainted with their staff. Since they have computerized records of your earlier prescriptions, errors are less likely to occur and more easily detected. Checking your prescription bottles against your personal list of medications before leaving the pharmacy will reduce the chances of errors by the drug store. Research shows we're all capable of errors, and pharmacies are no exception.

Within the past two years there has been a greater emphasis by health plans to have their subscribers send away for long term prescription drugs. This practice has reduced the cost of prescription drugs to the patient since copays are reduced or sometimes eliminated. It has also saved patients a monthly trip to their local pharmacy. The down side to this practice is that it has severely restricted the choices patients are given. Medications are dispensed by these long distance pharmacies primarily based on contracts that guarantee good prices to your health plan. A medication's effectiveness or its side effect profile may be a secondary consideration. Thus, sometimes these alternative drugs may be close to what your physician wanted to prescribe, yet not exactly what he had in mind. These mail away pharmacies attempt to provide comparable drugs that are close but not exactly the same; just as red delicious apples are sometimes replaced by macintosh. Physicians as well as patients are often coerced into going along with the program or face extensive amounts of red tape to alter a pharmacy's preferred selections.

The latest wrinkle in the pharmacy wars involves the sale of drugs over the Internet. The Internet can be convenient but drugs may be sold illegally by online pharmacies not licensed or properly certified. Many online pharmacies are illegally dispensing drugs without a prescription. If an online pharmacy is operating illegally, who is to say that their products meet FDA (Food and Drug Administration) standards; illegal drugs may be of poor quality or even expired.

A recent investigation turned up over 80 Internet sites selling Viagra (the anti-impotence drug) without a prescription. Taking drugs without a prescription suggests that people who do so, have not been properly evaluated by a physician. Without proper screening, these patients may be at risk and could suffer a major complication or side effect from a drug they believe to be safe. Most medications are safe when used within proper guidelines established through research and clinical investigation. Any prescription drug not properly prescribed and dispensed could result in dire consequences by the user. The law requires that prescription drugs be prescribed by licensed

170

practitioners who are knowledgeable about their patient's medical problems.

When possible, medications should be purchased from local pharmacies. This may sound old fashioned but building rapport with your pharmacist has its benefits. For convenience and as a cost savings, medications can be purchased through the mail from legitimate pharmacies recommended by your insurance plan. There is little doubt that Internet pharmacies will become more popular. Careful scrutiny by patients must be the rule in dealing with Internet pharmacies until regulations are in place to monitor and eliminate illegitimate vendors.

Chapter 36

Generic Drugs Vs. Name Brand and Other Medication Issues

Potential problems are associated with medication usage, whether one uses generic or name brand medications. Many issues concerning the appropriate use of antibiotics are being discussed and studied worldwide now that we are recognizing the rapid evolution of resistant organisms. Bacteria resistant to antibiotics are interfering with the satisfactory treatment of infectious diseases. This chapter will touch upon some of those problems.

Generic versus Name Brand Medication

Many patients have questions about the use of generic drugs versus the use of a brand name product. This is a frequent question heard in medical offices. According to rules or regulations established under Section 505 of the Federal Food, Drug, and Cosmetic Act, generic drugs need to be bioequivalent to brand name drugs. Bioequivalent drugs are those that display comparable bioavailability. Bioavailability is the rate and extent to which drugs are absorbed by the body becoming *available* for use at the "sight of action" in the body when studied under experimental conditions. Thus, how one drug compares to another in its effects on the heart, the kidneys or any other target organ reflects its bioavailability.

Comparable drugs must fall into a certain range of effectiveness. The Food and Drug Administration (FDA) regulations specify that if two drugs whose rate and extent of absorption differ within a range of between a - 20% and a +25%, they are generally considered bioeqiuvalent. The use of this rule from the FDA's "orange book," "is based on a medical decision that, *for most drugs*, a -20% / +25% difference in the concentration of the active ingredient in blood will not be clinically significant." However, as one can see, the regulations refer to *most drugs* and it does not refer to *all drugs*. For some drugs that may alter one's blood pressure, heart rate, nervous system function, or other important bodily functions, this degree of variation may be too generous.

The FDA's regulations also state that "When such differences are important in the care of a particular patient, it may be appropriate for the prescribing physician to require that a particular brand be dispensed as a medical necessity." The recent regulations of many health insurance plans, however, require that drugs be dispensed either as generics or from lists of drugs located in your insurance company's medication formulary should you hope to be reimbursed by your health plan. Lately, even when a drug is necessary, it's become a paperwork nightmare for physicians to dispense drugs outside the recommendations of your health plan. As you can see, the current actions of some insurance companies appear to be in conflict within the spirit of the F.D.A.'s "orange book" recommendations, allowing your doctor a free hand in prescribing medications as he sees fit.

When one carefully considers the above -20%/ +25% rule, a surprising effect becomes readily apparent. Consider the following: diazepam, a generic form of the name brand Valium, could be as much as twenty percent weaker or as much as twenty-five percent stronger than the name brand. Generic A could in turn vary from generic B by a total spread of forty-five percent and still be within F.D.A. guidelines. This allowable variation in generic medications may become important to a patient if during one month they are on generic drug A, and the next month when their prescription is refilled, they are given generic drug B. Effectiveness and side effects will vary with the strength of your medications. Most generic medications will not vary so widely, but the possibility remains.

Most physicians would agree that one of the most important drugs usually prescribed by name brand is Coumadin, a medication used to lower the risk of blood clotting in patients with various vascular or heart disorders. Controlling the "blood thinning" effects of Coumadin, which can easily be altered by a patient's diet, is a challenge in its own right; trying to deal with

174

the potential variations of one generic drug versus another complicates matters even further. Coumadin, though potentially dangerous, is used to prevent even more dangerous consequences. It should be used with the utmost care, and only under close surveillance by your physician. In fact Coumadin's ability to alter blood clotting is often evaluated by blood testing every one to two weeks. Using a generic form of Coumadin may add another variable, complicating the entire therapeutic program. Most authorities agree that Coumadin is an example of a drug in which generic substitutions are usually not acceptable.

Several other products fall into this category, though improved manufacturing techniques may be diminishing the need for the overzealous use of proprietary or name brand medications. The appropriate use of prescription medications with the potential of serious side effects and drug interactions must remain in the hands of physicians and must not be delegated to insurance companies to control.

When it comes to the use of newer name brand medications, consider a few additional thoughts. Many modern name brand drugs are designed with special release mechanisms, providing for a slow, controlled effect. This technology allows a medication to be slowly absorbed by the body, often bypassing the stomach where irritation often will occur. Medications like these will then be absorbed by the small intestine, reducing some side effects that could have otherwise occurred. These slow-release drugs are expensive to design and manufacture. Due to their prolonged effects, these drugs require fewer doses and reduce the hill-and-valley effect that many generic drugs may exhibit on our systems.

Some patients have difficulty swallowing medications and are tempted to chew them. In the case of most slow-release drugs this could result in unfavorable side effects since the tablet was not intended to be chewed. Some tablets are scored down the center with a grove that allows the tablet to be broken in half. With these types of medications it would be acceptable to split the tablets to allow for more easy swallowing or for divided dosing. This can best be accomplished by the use of a pill splitter available at the drug store for three to four dollars. The traditional approach of using a knife to split a tablet will often shatter the tablet into unequal portions. This method would be acceptable if you intend to use the entire tablet, but should be avoided when only half tablet use is intended. Unscored tablets should not be split without consulting your physician.

Medication in the form of capsules should never be cut, broken nor pulled in half. One of my patients once decided to separate the halves of a capsule and then attempted to divide the enclosed powder into equal portions. I had reduced her dosage on a new prescription and she didn't want to waist the older medication. This of course should never be attempted for several reasons. The contents of a capsule could stain one's teeth, could cause a bitter or painful response within the mouth, a coughing or choking sensation within the throat or some other unexpected unsatisfactory effect. These drugs are meant to be swallowed intact and not altered in some other way.

Having said that, there are rare exceptions to the above rule. Prevacid, a drug available by prescription and in capsule form, is used to suppress stomach acid secretion. It is the only medication in its class that can be opened. The capsule can be pulled apart and its contents sprinkled on apple sauce, pudding, cottage cheese and yogurt without changing the effect of the medication nor the taste of the food to which it has been applied. It can also be placed in orange, apple, grape, cranberry and tomato juices and swallowed or passed down a gastric tube into a patient's stomach. This approach is helpful for patients with swallowing difficulties, especially the elderly or those in nursing homes. Check with your physician for a list of foods or liquids that can be used in this manner with Prevacid should the need arise.

It is worthwhile remembering that many name brand medications were either expensive to develop or expensive to manufacture. Good medication costs money. Better medication costs more money. The best drugs are the best drugs for a reason.

Many insurance companies actively discriminate against the use of name brands by forcing patients to pay a premium for them. Under a worst-case scenario, sometimes the insurance companies will not pay for any part of a prescription if the drug chosen by your physician is not on their list of preferred choices. If your physician notes on your prescription that only a name brand be prescribed, then his/her order will usually be binding. In different states, there are different ways to note on a prescription that a drug that has been prescribed should be *dispensed as written.* This phrase means a generic drug should not be substituted for the brand that was specified. Your physician will commonly be required to write a letter, fax a message or even call your insurance company to explain why a name brand drug is best for you. Unfortunately, these attempts don't always work.

For obvious reasons, this approach to the delivery of medical care is not practical for the majority of prescriptions. Most physicians, when possible, prescribe generic drugs to aid in controlling costs – hoping to play their part in reducing the escalation of higher insurance premiums. It is interesting to note that under certain circumstances, pharmacies may also prefer to dispense generic drugs. They often realize a higher profit margin when dispensing generic instead of name brand medications.

Other times name brand drugs should be your first choice. Whenever starting a new medication, it is wise at first to choose a name brand over a generic drug. If the name brand drug fails to achieve a beneficial result, it is even less likely that a generic drug would be helpful. Should you experience good results through the use of a name brand medication, then later switching to a generic medication is worth trying for comparison purposes. If you begin with a generic drug and fail to achieve good results or experience adverse side effects, you cannot simply assume that the name brand would have performed in the same fashion.

Sometimes prescriptions, as written by your physician, may not allow you to switch to generic brands. Should long-term medication be required, request that your physician change how the prescription is written to allow for a generic brand to be tried on a trial basis. When possible, staying with an acceptable generic drug over the long run will save you money. When generic drugs do not work as well as a name brand, however,

177

you may not end up saving any money – considering the extra doctor's visits and time spent on experimentation. Remember, no two patients are alike. All patients have different needs, different metabolisms and different genetics, all of which impact on how drugs affect them. If you feel better when taking a name brand drug – experiencing superior results and fewer side effects – insist on having your physician prescribe it.

Patients Requesting Medications

According to a recent article in *The Medical Tribune*, December, 1999, doctors are more responsive to patient's requests for specific medications. Physicians are complying more than 30% of the time according to researchers at the University of Mississippi. Phone interviews with 199 primary care physicians from Ohio and Pennsylvania indicated that on average six patients per week asked about a particular drug and in 36% of the cases their physician prescribed it. Fueled by television, newspaper and magazine advertising, patients are requesting certain medications more aggressively and more frequently than in the past. In most cases, some degree of caution must be maintained when considering various media advertisements for prescription medications. Herman Abromowitz, MD, a member of the Board of Trustees of the American Medical Association said, " In all cases, the advertisement should refer patients to their physician for more information. The patient-physician relationship is paramount. If this makes my patients challenge my treatment plan, that's fine. The more informed the patient is, the better the patient is. There should be a dialogue between patients and the physician concerning their medication".

The Use of Multiple Medications

Many patients must take several medications. As you are prescribed new medications, you may find that some of them adversely interact with your current medications. When you are on several medications, one drug may even neutralize or

178

diminish the effectiveness of another. Some medications cannot be taken together. Some should be taken with food while others must be taken on an empty stomach. Some must be taken only in the evening while others should be taken only in the morning. The regular use of medication can be a complicated affair, requiring close cooperation on your part with your physician or pharmacist.

Carefully following the directions written on your medication container is a good practice. Physicians sometimes prescribe a medication to be taken every six hours. This implies two things. First, the medication should be taken as close as possible to a six-hour schedule. Because there are four six-hour increments within each day, the medicine should be taken four times within a twenty-four hour day. Many patients have said to me, "Oh, I only take three pills per day, scheduling one every six hours." They obviously forgot or ignored their nighttime dose. This practice could result in poor performance from medication requiring six-hour intervals. This problem has been more of an issue in the past. Most modern drugs need be taken only once or twice a day improving results and compliance.

After your physician has prescribed a medication, be sure to ask him to review common side effects that may occur. Recent studies indicate that two out of three physicians fail to review potential side effects. Should your physician forget, remember to ask about adverse consequences.

It is not uncommon for patients to be given by their doctor two and sometimes three new medicines at the same time. Should this occur, it is generally not wise to take all of them at the same time, unless specifically told to do so by your physician. It is best to select one medication first and take it. Then wait two or three hours before a second or third medication is tried. Should an adverse reaction occur when using a new medication, spacing the drug will allow a better opportunity for you to decide which medicine is the culprit. If you had taken all of your new medications with the very first dose, and an adverse event occurred, it might be impossible to know which medicine was the cause.

Lastly and most importantly you must remember to take your medications as directed and on time. If you're on several medications, it's best to purchase an inexpensive seven-day plastic pill dispenser. These unique pill boxes have seven individual compartments, each holding a full day's worth of medication. Checking your dispenser daily will provide an accurate method to monitor your medication usage. Placing your dispenser in a routinely-visited location will allow you to notice it each day. Location, location, location are the three most important words to remember when medications are needed. Many of these containers are not childproof, so users must practice discretion and good safety precautions. Medications should never be left within a child's reach.

In 1996, there were 2.2 million poisonings reported according to Dr. Litovitz, *American Journal of Emergency Medicine* 15: 447. Another 1.5 million human poisonings were probably not reported. Boys generally exceed girls in exposures. Eighty-five percent of poisonings are unintended leaving fifteen percent intentional. Local poison control centers will care for eighty percent of these poisonings at home over the telephone. Most exposures involve children less than six years of age. The most common exposures in this order include cosmetics, cleaning substances, analgesics such as acetaminophen or ibuprofen, plants, cough and cold preparations and foreign bodies such as tiny button sized batteries. It is of interest to note, according to Dr. Litovitz, as reported in *Pediatrics* 89: 999, 1992, that the most common cause of death from drug poisoning is due to taking iron in some form. He also found that the number one cause of death from non pharmaceutical poisoning is from exposure to hydrocarbons such as kerosene, lighter fluids and furniture polish.

Parents cannot be too careful about keeping medications and other dangerous chemicals in secure places.

In summary, the prescribing, dispensing and use of medications is a complicated affair. One must have the utmost respect for their medications. Modern drugs are often life sustaining if not life saving. Used carelessly or not at all can prove to be very dangerous. Remain informed about your medications and consult your physician or pharmacist about side effects or adverse reactions should they occur. Do not make independent decisions on how to manage your medications.

Chapter 37

The Antibiotic Crisis

The Evolution of Antibiotic Resistance

In recent years a medical crisis has resulted from the overuse of antibiotics. Over time, bacteria develop internal mechanisms to defeat or destroy antibiotics they have been exposed to. This process, which eventually makes many antibiotics useless in the war against fighting infections, is referred to as the development of antibiotic resistance. This is not a new problem, but it is gradually becoming more severe. The situation is so serious that only the newest antibiotics are effective in the treatment of some difficult infections. Bacterial resistance can vary not only from city to city, but often from hospital to hospital, as well. All physicians are aware of this problem and are trying to deal with the situation.

Bacterial resistance to antibiotics began after World War II, and it has flourished from the overuse or incorrect use of antibiotics over the years. One of the biggest causes of the evolution of antibiotic resistance is due to patients who fail to complete a full course of antibiotics. A short or inadequate course of antibiotics will kill off weaker bacteria, leaving the stronger ones to multiply. When your physician gives you a prescription for antibiotics, be sure to take the entire amount prescribed. Failure to do so can result in a resistant infection occurring on the heels of your original infection. Keeping unfinished prescriptions of antibiotics for future self-medication can be equally dangerous. Some patients will self-medicate a new infection with a few leftover antibiotics. Worse than that, before seeing their physician a few patients will take leftover antibiotics given to them from friends or relatives. This behavior is never a good idea. After failing in their own attempts at a cure, these patients will often later visit their doctor for help.

Unfortunately, the premature use of antibiotics can interfere with needed diagnostic tests, often further complicating a patient's problem. It is also possible that a few pills altered the physical appearance of the disease, thus hindering a physician's ability to diagnose it.

In an article entitled "The Antibiotic Crisis," published in the November, 1998, issue of the medical journal *Hippocrates,* Peter Jaret notes that "Experts insist that bacterial strains resistant to all known antibiotics are just around the corner. The first such cases have already shown up in U.S. and Asian hospitals." He then asks, "Is there still time for doctors and their patients to avert disaster?"

Several strains of common bacteria are already untreatable, including some strains of enterococcus, tuberculosis and Pseudomonas aeruginosa. Authorities believe a strain of staph (staphylococcus aureus) will soon be fully resistant to all antibiotics.

According to David Bell, assistant to the director of the National Center for Infectious Diseases, "We now have a situation where most of the pathogens (organisms) that cause serious human disease are resistant to at least one and often several of the drugs used to treat them."

A bacterial population can double in size every twenty minutes, resulting in many opportunities for genetic mutations and the inevitable development of antibiotic resistance. The problem is partially due to the fact that forty percent of antibiotics given to livestock and other animals are done so to stimulate growth rather then to fight infections. It has been shown that as resistance emerges, whether it be from animal or from human use, the resistant genes are from a shared gene pool. Therefore, the same resistant bacteria can be found in farm animals and humans alike. A new bill before congress, HR 3266, was introduced in November 1999, by Rep. Sherrod Brown (D, Ohio), that would ban the use of antibiotics for livestock unless the manufacturer proves that such use would not increase resistance in bacteria that could harm humans.

Les Gara, an attorney from Anchorage, Alaska, was quoted in the *Hippocrates* article as saying that " It surprised me to learn just now that you're supposed to finish the whole (prescription) of antibiotics. Until (you) told me, I didn't know that if you take half the pills the illness could come back, or that the germs could get resistant to them. I can't say for sure that a doctor never told me to take them all, but I don't remember it. Maybe it's a matter of communication: If I had ever been told the reason for taking them, I know I would have."

A large part of the antibiotic crisis is reflected by a 1997 study indicating that doctors are ten times more likely to prescribe antibiotics when patients expect them. Patients feel their illness is not taken seriously if antibiotics are not prescribed. According to David Bell from The Center for Disease Control in Atlanta, "Doctors are under enormous pressure" to prescribe antibiotics. Under the time constraints of managed care, along with patients' preconceived notions about antibiotics, it is simply easier for many physicians to prescribe them rather than to review the reasons not to. In my experience, after I have detailed the reasons for not giving an antibiotic, patients still insist on them by saying, "Only this time; I have to be well for work (for my trip, for my exams, for my anniversary)."

The antibiotic crisis will continue to escalate should we not respect the forces of nature. All of us have a role to play in protecting each other from the future consequences of the incorrect or over zealous use of antibiotics.

Chapter 38

When, if Ever, to Discontinue Antibiotics

Despite the warnings in the previous chapter, sometimes antibiotics unexpectedly must be discontinued. There are three common reasons for the legitimate discontinuation of antibiotics. The first is associated with unsatisfactory side effects, such as nausea and vomiting, which may require discontinuation. The second reason for discontinuation is an allergic reaction – as indicated by hives, a widespread rash, or the sudden onset of respiratory distress. The third reason is that an antibiotic may not work effectively.

In all cases, *always* contact your physician before stopping your course of treatment. Many patients incorrectly attribute rashes and various symptoms to medications, when in fact their perceived side effect is not due to the medication. Calling your doctor and asking him or her to analyze your rash over the phone may lead to diagnostic mistakes. If you develop a rash, it is best to be seen by your physician.

With the limited number of effective antibiotics on the market, it is unwise to incriminate a medication as the cause of an allergic reaction until you have seen your physician. Should you not pursue a definitive answer from your physician about whether or not the antibiotic was to blame for your reaction, you may never be able to use the antibiotic again. This would limit your options for the treatment of future infectious illnesses.

You can help fight the war against the development of resistant bacteria that do not respond to current antibiotics by working with your physician and learning about the proper use of these life saving medications. For more information about antibiotic resistance, contact the Alliance for the Prudent Use of Antibiotics at (617) 636-0966.

Chapter 39

Phoning in Prescription Refills

Your physician's office receives many calls from patients requesting refills on their prescription medication. On the surface, this practice appears to save time and money for all involved. In fact, however, it has many potential drawbacks. Refilling prescriptions over the phone is a time-consuming venture. A busy medical practice may receive ten or more calls each day requesting refills of medications. The process of determining whether or not your refills can be allowed requires several steps. First, your medical record needs to be pulled from record stacks so your physician can determine when your last office visit took place. Then your doctor must review your current medication list, as well as your active medical problems. Often, managed care drug formularies must be reviewed for new regulations regarding your prescription benefits. Requesting a prescription refill may appear to be a simple demand, but it can easily take ten to fifteen minutes of your physician's time. If he is extremely busy, he may even forget or be unable to carry out all of these steps.

There are several reasons why visiting your physician is a wise idea when the time comes to refill medications. All prescriptions must be monitored at regular intervals varying in length from drug to drug. All prescription drugs, though necessary to improve function or sustain life are also inherently dangerous. If medications did not have the potential to cause harm, they would be available to the average patient on an over-the-counter basis and thus not require a prescription.

Physician monitoring will help determine if the medication is performing as intended; have important goals or effects been achieved? If not, what can be done about it? Medications will alter our physiology sometimes only detectable by physical examination and analysis of your vital signs including pulse, blood pressure and respiration.

189

Good medications are not without their potential problems. Many medications require periodic blood testing to evaluate for possible adverse consequences that can result in damage to vital organs such as the liver, kidneys, heart or nervous system. Most patients also benefit from baseline blood studies obtained before starting new medications. Proper study protocols and recommendations will often be incorporated into your routine office visits. If organ damage has gone undetected for too long of a period, then the effects may not be reversible. Office checkups will usually reveal adverse changes usually reversible once a medication has been discontinued.

Sometimes medications need not be discontinued. Frequently the dose of the medication is either increased or reduced. Small changes can result in improved performance or rid patients of unsatisfactory side effects. During your office visit your physician may determine that your medication has to be discontinued. When your physician determines that a medication is unacceptable, then other medication will be required to replace your current drug.

You may need to change medications when their usefulness has run out or newer, safer and more effective products become available. More frequently than not, most patients will have to be continued on some form of medication for life since few conditions are cured; it should be remembered that for practical purposes good management is often equal to a cure.

Most physicians write a prescription for a given length of time to encourage patients to return for follow-up-visits. Regular visits will ensure proper and thorough evaluations and lessen the risks and complications of chronic medication use. Drugs without risks are usually of minimal value and certainly cannot be trusted for the management of most life-threatening or chronic disorders. Effective medications work because they are altering your body's chemistry, and these alterations must be checked. If your physician repeatedly refills your medications without close supervision, it may be time to consider either a change of medication or a change of physician, since neither may be doing you much good.

With only a few exceptions, most medications require regular office visits generally on a six-month schedule. Older or more sickly patients, and those on multiple prescriptions, may need to be seen every three to four months. If you have recently started a new medication and it is working well, you still need a follow-up visit to evaluate for side effects that may not be apparent to you, but would be detectable by your physician. As you can see, simply calling in for refills without proper evaluation is a practice that must be strongly discouraged. Telephone refills result in more errors than traditional office visits and tend to lull people into the belief that they are doing fine.

Breakthroughs related to the use of new medications are occurring at break-neck speed. There is rarely a day that goes by that a new medication does not become available for patient use. You may be the recipient of that good fortune. However, phone call medical practice will not offer you the opportunity to discover newer and better therapies. Most likely, your physician will be reluctant to discuss new concepts or treatments over the phone.

"You are only a phone call away," does not often make sense in the complicated world of modern medical care. Shortcuts are exactly that. You will pay a price one way or the other if you are not diligent about receiving world-class care. Demand it, even if it has not been offered. Ask your doctor if there are any tests required to see if your medications are working safely.

If you are worried about the costs of follow-up visits to see if you are doing well, you shouldn't be. Usually your insurance company will cover the cost of periodic maintenance office visits. The cost of paying for reasonable testing to detect for dangerous side effects to vital organs such as the liver and kidneys from medication can be charged under the use of a dangerous drug code. Proper blood testing and monitoring is an acceptable practice covered by your insurance policy. It is cheaper, safer and more convenient over the long haul for your insurance company to pay for liver and kidney tests than it would be to perform organ transplants. Patients with known liver or kidney disease need to be monitored even more closely than those with normal organ function.

One might then say, "If all of this is necessary, may the drugs be too dangerous for common use?" When prescribed and used properly, medications are generally not dangerous, and for the vast majority of patients they do much more good than harm. Being cautious is simply a matter of common sense and self-preservation. Automobiles are potentially dangerous, but is that a reason not to drive?

In summary, if your prescription medication needs to be refilled, it may be wiser to schedule an office visit than to simply call in for more medication. If proper follow-up evaluations were not necessary, your physician would simply provide prescriptions for you that could run for years. Obviously, this does not make sense, and good medical management requires regular office visits.

Chapter 40

Reading the Small Print: Medication Package Inserts

The small, tightly folded wads of paper written in small print accompanying samples of medication are provided by pharmaceutical manufacturers for informational purposes. They provide pharmacists and physicians with detailed information about the chemistry and pharmacological properties associated with the enclosed medication. These slips of paper explain the mechanism of action (how the drug is believed to work), the side effects, precautions, drug interactions and other important facts. Much of this information can be difficult for a layperson to interpret. As a result, most large pharmacies also provide an abbreviated, simplified account written in layman's terms for patients to read. Many pharmacists will also provide a few details or salient features they believe are important for you to understand.

It is important to recognize that the primary reason why pharmacies provide this information is to reduce their risk of litigation when something unexpectedly goes wrong. The second reason is to educate patients about the medicine and its uses. Here is where problems may arise. Side effects and complications of medications may be highlighted on these handouts. Patients reading the risk profiles of their prescription drugs often become frightened and decide not to use the medication. Your doctor, however, has determined before prescribing a new medication that the benefits of taking the medicine outweigh the potential risks or side effects. The failure to take a medicine as prescribed is nearly always riskier than the potential harm that could result from its use. Remember that most serious complications are rare, or the Food and Drug Administration would not permit marketing of the drug. Medications are withdrawn from the market if after widespread use they are proven to be unacceptable. Only a small percent of medications are withdrawn annually from the market.

Many minor side effects can occur from the use of medication, but most are rapidly reversible once the medication has been stopped. Aspirin, which is available without a prescription, is actually more dangerous than most currently available prescription drugs. Since aspirin has been available for generations without a prescription, the public would not tolerate a change in its status. If aspirin were to be brought out as a new product today, its many side effects – including potentially serious stomach bleeding – would require it to be dispensed only with a prescription.

Sometimes pharmacists will give advice or instructions that differ from that of your physician. Contact your physician immediately if this happens. Once in a while, your physician has made an error. More often than not, however, there is a satisfactory explanation to your questions or concerns. Your physician usually has a solid reason for prescribing the medication as he did. Many medications may be used for medical problems and purposes not listed on the pharmacist's handout. Doctors will use medications as they see fit, sometimes stepping outside of standard guidelines published by the FDA. Most physicians are familiar with the latest research, which may have revealed new uses for drugs that are not always found in your package insert. When a medication is used to treat a condition that has not been approved by the FDA, the dosage of the medication may differ from what is listed in the package insert. Pharmacists are usually not familiar with new uses for current medications, since this is not one of their primary responsibilities. Once again, if you're uncertain or fearful about the use of a medication, contact your physician. An educated patient is much more likely to take medications appropriately. Patients must understand their health problems and all medications required to manage them, and physicians are responsible for explaining why and how medicines should be used.

Chapter 41

The Formulary

One of the more recent requirements of many health care management plans is that patients use medications from a preferred list to save money and reduce their copay. Medications not appearing on your medical insurance preferred list or formulary may only be partially covered. Sometimes they are not covered at all, requiring you to shoulder the entire cost of a particular medication. When your doctor believes there is no reasonable alternative medication for your medical problem, he can request that your health plan review your case to determine if alternative medications are warranted. Arranging for special treatment such as this, requires a lot of extra work for your physician and his office staff. Unless your needs clearly warrant a specific drug, it may not be practical for your physician to petition your insurance company for a change of medication.

Most insurance companies provide their customers with a formulary – or list of preferred medications. Bringing a copy of your preferred list of medications along with you for your office visit is a big help for your physician, since he may not have a current edition. Your physician will then have the opportunity to select medications from your approved list, saving money both for you and your insurance company. On occasion, newer or less frequently used medications may not be listed in your formulary. Sometimes a physician will have to select a drug that is not approved by your insurance company's formulary. With proper documentation, insurance companies will generally agree to assist their patients with their needs.

SECTION V: SPECIAL TESTS AND EXAMS

Chapter 42

Office Procedures:
When Should They Be Done and How to Prepare for Them

Physicians are capable of performing a variety of procedures in their office, either to diagnose or to treat a variety of diseases. The procedures or tests that can be performed vary widely from specialist to specialist. They are generally well tolerated, though they are not necessarily pain-free. After a test, a patient will generally be able to leave their physician's office and resume their usual activities.

The most important thing to know about any procedure is why it is being performed and what are its possible consequences. Some procedures are associated with significant risk, but in the right hands they are generally safe. Having a clear picture of what needs to be done is vital for several reasons. First, tests will have to be repeated every few years throughout your life. Also, a person who has had a terrible experience from a test or procedure will be less likely to repeat the same procedure later, when it may be even more important to do so.

If there are proper indications for performing a test, the advantages will most likely significantly outweigh any risks. The key word here is *indications*, which refers to a list of reasons why a procedure should be done. Is the procedure being done to diagnose a problem? Is it being done to solve a problem? Sometimes the procedure is done for both reasons. What will be gained by successful completion of the test? What will be lost if the test isn't completed? Where is the procedure done?

Other questions that you will want answered include the following: How is the procedure performed? What are possible complications of the procedure? How are the complications handled should any occur? What preparations are required beforehand?

You need to be prepared to ask the right questions. You also need to be prepared to accept the consequences of not having a test or procedure done should you refuse. After a test has been fully justified, you will usually be much more accepting – or even insistent – on following through with it. Too many patients have procedures performed without adequate knowledge or understanding of the risks or goals to be achieved. Some patients accept all tests without questioning and then become upset when complications occur.

After your physician has revealed all possible complications of a procedure, you must then give it careful thought. If you are not sure what to do, go home and sleep on it. If a specialist other than your primary care physician is performing the test, and you remain confused or concerned, then you should discuss your feelings with your family doctor. Asking friends or relatives about a test is generally not one's best option, since their experiences might not provide a reliable comparison.

Once you have decided to follow through with a test, proper preparation is mandatory. Many examinations of the abdomen or intestinal tract will require the use of laxatives, enemas, or other preparations required to clean out the lower colon or large bowel to achieve the desired information. Not following instructions will result in cancellation of the test or unsatisfactory results, often requiring a repeat performance.

Remember also to discuss the results or outcome of your test with the physician who performed it. Taking notes for future review is a good practice. Many patients return to my office for follow-up care prior to the arrival of test results, and these notes help us to discuss possible outcomes. If the results of the tests are not offered, request them and record them on paper before leaving the premises. Not all test results will be immediately available, but the outcome of procedures such as colonoscopy (viewing the colon with a special scope) , gastroscopy (viewing the stomach with a special scope) are usually known immediately after the exam is completed. This may not be true of x-ray studies, however, which require detailed interpretation by a radiologist.

Some physicians may try to review test results with a patient who is still sedated by an anesthetic given to them prior to their procedure. In this case, you may not remember what your physician says. If you know ahead of time that you will be sedated, you may want to bring a trusted friend or relative to review the test results with your physician. If bringing someone is not possible, do not be embarrassed to contact your physician and request a written report of the procedure after you return home. After every test or procedure has been performed, your physician will record the findings in your medical record. It is not difficult to produce a brief description of test results for you or for other physicians who might need it.

The Detection of Colon and Rectal Cancer: Stool Studies

Colon cancer is the second most common form of cancer in the US, exceeded only by lung cancer. Over 130,000 cases of colon cancer are diagnosed each year in the US. Unfortunately many of these cancers are diagnosed later than they have to be resulting in over 50,000 deaths **annually** from a disease that can be detected in its early stages. To put this disease into perspective, 50,000 American service men died during the Vietnam War. Katy Couric's husband Jay Monahan, died of this disease at age 42. Each year near the anniversary of his death, she reminds her television audience about the need for proper screening for colon cancer. She as well as many experts refer to colonoscopy as the "gold standard" when used for the early detection of colon cancer. This test will be reviewed in-depth later on.

There are a few tests that most of us do not wish to talk about but they are necessary in that they can prove life saving. Fortunately colon cancer is readily diagnosed by proper tests. All patients aged fifty and over should be monitored on an annual basis for the occurrence of non-visible blood in their stool – a possible sign of colon cancer. Stool specimens can be collected at home for this purpose. This can be accomplished by requesting from your doctor three cardboard cards, each having small wells where samples of your stool can be deposited. These stool samples can be tested in your doctor's office to detect the presence of blood. Any amount of blood passed in one's stool must be taken seriously. The good news, however, is that in most cases blood in your stool does not indicate the presence of colon cancer. During the week prior to obtaining stool specimens, one must avoid red meats, vitamin C, citrus fruits, aspirin and similar drugs such as ibuprofen. These substances can cause a false positive test. For example, if you are using aspirin for pain relief, it may cause bleeding from your stomach. In some patients the lining of their stomach can be inflamed by even small amounts of aspirin resulting in trace amounts of bleeding. If blood is found in your stool, additional tests may be needed to determine its cause.

Blood tests alone are usually not enough to determine the presence of cancer, however. In many cases, your doctor will order what is called a sigmoidoscopy to look inside your colon. Small growths referred to as polyps may start to grow from the internal wall of one's colon. In many cases these are benign. Some, unfortunately, are cancerous. These small tumors, or polyps, do not always bleed, even when cancerous. Therefore, stool tests for blood may be negative even when one has early changes that may be the precursors of colon cancer. These stool tests are used for preliminary screening. Some patients are considered to be at greater risk for cancer such as those over the age of fifty or those with a family history of colon cancer. They will require additional procedures every few years to detect cancer even when their stool tests are negative for blood.

A sigmoidoscopy is performed with a flexible, fiber-optic, tube-like rubber instrument that is smaller in diameter than the small finger on your hand. Though it is small in diameter, it is between sixty to sixty-five centimeters or two and one half feet in length. The procedure can be performed after a patient's lower bowel, or colon, has been properly cleaned out through the use of enemas or special liquids taken by mouth.

Usually a clear liquid diet 18 to 24 hours before the exam is required. You should not drink opaque liquids, such as milk. When the lower bowel, or colon, is to be examined, patients are most often given a prescription for a special liquid drink to be taken the night before the exam to clean out the intestinal track. Some patients may instead be given laxatives, while others are instructed in the use of enemas. Failure to follow correct instructions may result in cancellation of your test at the last minute, which is never a happy occurrence. If your lower bowel is not properly prepared, the test may be inaccurate or even entail unnecessary risks during the use of endoscopes to examine your bowel. Most medical facilities provide written or visual instructions before your test; make sure that you understand and follow these instructions.

It is also advisable to review with your physician or his or her staff the necessary preparations for your procedure, the techniques that will be used during your test, and potential complications that you might experience during or after the test. Patients often complain that they receive inadequate instructions, but it is up to you to take the initiative and request that you receive proper instructions. And when you receive written instructions, read them carefully. Many patients lose written instructions, or read them and then do not follow them. Some patients believe they know what to do, and then fail to follow current instructions or recommendations.

Now let us consider how the exam is actually performed. The procedure usually begins with you lying on your side after being place on an exam table. Then you are asked to pull both of your legs up towards your abdomen placing you in a fetal like position. Additional comfort can be achieved by placing a pillow between your knees. You will then be covered with a drape to provide some warmth and privacy. After being properly positioned on the exam table, the lubricated tip of the sigmoidoscope is gently inserted into your rectum. Under visual observation the scope is slowly passed through the rectum and advanced into the lower sigmoid colon. Through the scope, your physician will examine the inner walls of the colon, looking for hemorrhoids, defects, tumors, constrictions or any other abnormalities that may occur. Sometimes the colon is not dilated enough for proper visualization, and small amounts of air may be administered to inflate the colon. This can cause some cramping, so as little air as possible is administered. Discomfort can be minimized when diazepam, an anxiety-relieving drug and muscle relaxer, is taken one hour before the procedure. If you are relaxed, the procedure will be less uncomfortable, easier to perform and more quickly completed. In my experience, the use of a single tablet of diazepam can reduce by fifty percent the time needed to complete the procedure.

The most serious complication in the performance of sigmoidoscopy is the unlikely possibility of perforation of the colon wall with the scope. In the right hands, this complication is extremely rare, occurring about once in ten thousand procedures. I have done almost one thousand sigmoidoscopies, and not one has resulted in any significant complications. In about twenty-two percent of my patients, I have found important problems – including hemorrhoids, polyps, cancers, colitis and other bowel diseases.

Most patients over the age of fifty should have sigmoidoscopies performed every four to five years, even if their stool studies for blood are normal. If a patient has a positive test for blood in their stool, a more comprehensive test known as colonoscopy, which employs the use of a longer scope, may be needed. The colonoscope is identical to a sigmoidoscope, only twice as long. People having colonoscopies performed are generally well sedated to eliminate discomfort that would be more likely to occur when using the longer scope. They are then placed in a special procedure room to have the test performed.

Patients having a family history of colon cancer should begin colonoscopies at the age of forty. If polyps are found at any age, then colonoscopies may be needed more frequently. Finding polyps in their early stages and removing them through the use of a surgical colonoscope will prevent death from colon cancer. Early detection is possible if patients participate in an active way by reminding doctors of the need for this test should it have been overlooked.

Sometimes routine sigmoidoscopies may not be covered by your health insurance. Nevertheless, having it done every four to five years can reap great benefits, by the early detection of colon cancer. Early detection can be life saving and will also avoid the need for more complicated procedures or chemotherapy.

Chapter 43

Preparation for Medical Testing

Many tests, whether they are performed in your physician's office or at a local hospital, will require some form of preparation before the test can be conducted. Informed consent is provided by physicians or their staff should there be risk associated with any test or procedure. Some physicians will require your signature on an informed consent form before undergoing complicated or potentially dangerous tests. The purpose of this form is to describe the test and its possible consequences.

As noted earlier, some tests more than others incur a certain degree of risk. Another example of this might be an exercise stress test conducted by walking on a treadmill while electronically monitoring your heart. As the test proceeds, patients are asked to do more work by increasing the angle of the platform or by increasing the rate of speed of the treadmill. Under increasing physical duress, electrical evidence indicating the presence of coronary heart disease is sought. During the performance of an exercise stress test, on rare occasions, a patient not known to have dangerous coronary artery disease may suffer a blackout or a heart attack.

Adverse consequences can occur with some tests, and it is now becoming commonplace to delineate the adverse consequences of a test – along with its potential benefits – on a slip of paper for a patient to review. Please carefully review the "informed consent form." Often forms have more detailed information than your physician may have provided. The form will describe how the test is conducted, information that will be gathered by the test, and possible complications resulting from the test. When you feel comfortable with the contents of the consent form, you will be asked to sign it. If you are uncomfortable with any aspects of the test or the form, discuss these issues with your physician before signing.

Other tests require some preparation on your part beforehand. Sometimes the preparation is relatively uncomplicated, such as fasting a certain number of hours before the test is conducted. Preparation for other tests can be more complicated. Make sure you understand what is required of you; the better prepared you are, the more likely the test results will be accurate.

Blood, urine and throat testing are the most commonly performed tests. Some blood tests require a ten- to twelve-hour overnight fast to ensure accurate results. In these cases you fast the evening before your test, generally beginning at 9:00 p.m. As a general rule, drinking water, black coffee or black tea without cream or sugar will not interfere with your testing. It is usually advisable to take your morning medications for high blood pressure, heart disease and most other conditions even when your blood is to be drawn. Failure to take your medications as prescribed can be harmful. A common exception pertains to patients with diabetes. Diabetics who will not be eating on their usual schedule will have to withhold diabetic medications that if taken without food could result in lower than healthy blood sugars. All diabetic patients must check with their physician before testing to determine which medications, if any, must be withheld.

Fasting overnight before an early morning appointment may be worth considering if you are uncertain whether or not your physician may request blood testing. Some patients prior to their visit may decide unknown to their physcian that blood testing is desirable. Those of you considering the possibilty of requesting a test should also fast remembering not to eat after 9:00 PM. It is acceptable to have water, a cup of black coffee (no cream or sugar) or a cup of black tea in the morning before blood testing. These beverages will not adversely alter the test results. Without proper fasting, many tests will not be accurate. The most common tests requiring an overnight fast include blood sugar testing and cholesterol studies. Many patients take medications each morning for high blood pressure, diabetes and other chronic disorders. Should you remain uncertain about the use of medication before testing or before an office visit it is prudent to call your physician's office in advance for proper guidance.

Remember that in today's health insurance market, "routine" or wellness blood testing is often neither reimbursable nor covered by your insurer. That is not to say that these tests are not worthwhile. Many tests are valuable to you as an individual, but may not be necessarily viewed that way by your insurance carrier. Some commonly performed blood tests such as those which measure total cholesterol, blood sugar, and hemoglobin levels are so inexpensive that patients can easily pay for them. If you choose to proceed with tests that may not be approved, your physician may ask you to sign a waiver form specifying that your tests may not be reimbursable by your carrier. The cost of these tests then becomes your responsibility. The purpose of signing this waiver is to notify you that coverage may not be extended. Under some contract agreements between physicians and insurers, if a form has not been signed, your physician may not be able to bill you for screening or wellness tests. Therefore the tests will not be ordered.

Chapter 44

The Exam Room: Make Yourself Comfortable

Depending on the construction and furnishings of a facility, exam rooms may be comfortable or uncomfortable. They may be warm, cold or drafty. Patients are placed in rooms and then often left on an exam table, wearing various degrees of clothing or examination gowns, depending on what is to be done. This less-than-pleasant arrangement can be complicated by long waits, resulting in some degree of unhappiness – particularly for the acutely ill. Sitting on the end of an exam table for more than a few minutes can also prove troublesome when one is prone to back pain or back problems.

Many patients presume that once they have been placed on an exam table behind closed doors, they are stuck in an uncomfortable position for the duration. The tradition of exam table sitting may suit a physician's needs, but rarely serves the needs of the patient. You should, therefore, feel justified in adjusting your comfort level when your physician is not present. After all, you're paying for service, not for torture. If you feel cold, for instance, don't hesitate to grab the garment or coat that you wore to the office. Using it as a drape or cover-up over your examination gown can provide extra warmth until your doctor arrives. Likewise, if you are uncomfortable sitting on the table, alter your position or hop off the table and sit in a more comfortable chair.

For most routine office visits, the nurse places waiting patients on exam tables out of custom rather than need. You probably will not be criticized for finding a more comfortable arrangement. After your doctor has walked into the exam room, he will reposition or relocate you as the need arises. Don't forget, you're paying for service, not for aggravation. Bringing along a special book or magazine into the exam room to read while waiting may also be a good idea.

209

Chapter 45

Producing Specimens for Lab Analysis

Certain specimens are useful in diagnosing a variety of medical problems. One of the most useful specimens to evaluate is urine. For the urine sample to be usable, however, it must be properly collected. Bringing a random urine specimen from home sometimes suffices, but generally passing a fresh specimen at your doctor's office will provide a better sample. If your doctor asks you to bring in the first urine specimen you pass in the morning, then by all means follow those instructions. If no instructions have been given, it is better to arrive at your doctor's office with a full bladder of urine, rather than with a full bottle of urine. Urine samples more then twenty minutes old tend to lose some of their value, since bacteria will begin to multiply rapidly and alter the results. This can be a problem, particularly if you are seeing your doctor for treatment of a bladder or urinary tract infection. A freshly-passed urine specimen collected in the office and placed in a sterile container can be refrigerated for later use by lab or nursing personnel.

Specimens brought from home may be contaminated or inaccurate for several reasons. Improper containers, for example, can ruin or alter the results in a variety of urine tests. Some urine tests require a preservative to be placed in a freshly passed specimen to avoid natural deterioration of some of the urine's components. Passing a specimen at a laboratory facility or at your physician's office will reduce the chances of an unacceptable specimen and a return visit to provide another sample.

Many tests to insure accuracy require some forethought or preparation. For example, if you are seeing your doctor for a sore throat, gargling with an over-the-counter mouth wash or using medicinal lozenges before your office visit may alter the appearance of your throat and change the bacterial flora (the group of organisms naturally living there). This could hinder the physical examination of your throat and make the diagnosis of your illness more difficult.

In other words, when possible, visit your doctor without altering the part of your anatomy that may require examination. For example, a woman with a vaginal infection should not douche in the twenty-four hour period prior to a pelvic exam. She might want to douche to relieve her symptoms, but it may hamper the doctor's attempts to determine the cause of her infection. Vaginal specimens are obtained during an exam to be cultured or reviewed under a microscope, and douching before the exam may dilute or alter the characteristics of the secretions – thus reducing the chances for an accurate diagnosis.

Some patients with serious respiratory infections causing the production of mucous or phlegm may be asked to expectorate or cough up a specimen from their lungs. In this case the saliva from your mouth is not acceptable. The thicker or viscous mucous brought up with a deep cough from your bronchial tubes or lungs is the best source of organisms. Acquiring this type of material may allow for proper identification of the bacteria or organisms causing your illness. A properly-obtained specimen can be collected in a sterile container and then processed at a lab. Obtaining a good sputum specimen as described above is especially important when pneumonia or tuberculosis are a possibility.

Sometimes parents may be asked to bring in a diaper soiled from a child with persistent diarrhea. The appearance and characteristics of a patient's stool can give many clues when examined by a doctor or by a lab. A freshly-passed specimen in a child's diaper will provide more accurate results when one is trying to search for bacteria or parasites. The diaper should be folded over, placed in a sealed plastic bag and delivered as soon as possible to the laboratory your physician has selected.

Some labs provide containers with preservatives for the collection of stool or urine specimens. Sometimes a large amount of urine collected over a 24-hour period may be required to diagnose some conditions, and in these cases large specimen containers are available. Your physician or his laboratory will

212

provide the necessary instructions, containers, and materials required to collect needed specimens.

Properly following instructions will provide useful laboratory specimens that will assist your physician in correctly diagnosing your illness.

Chapter 46

The Throat Exam Can Be Tricky, but Not Impossible

Some portions of a physical exam are more annoying or uncomfortable than others. What appears to be a simple procedure for a medical professional may not be a pleasant experience for a patient. For example, one of the most common office exams is the throat exam. For many patients, this is an unpleasant and intimidating procedure, but with forethought, it need not be. If from past experience you are prone to gagging easily, simply ask the examiner to not use a tongue blade or depressor. It is often not necessary. Many practitioners are so conditioned to pulling out a tongue blade for a throat exam that we may forget the discomfort or gagging it causes for many adults and nearly all children.

Under most circumstances, a relaxed patient is fully capable of opening their mouth sufficiently for an adequate throat exam. In fact, a patient prone to gagging will tense up when they see a tongue depressor and will not open their mouth adequately, thus restricting the physician's view. Sensing this in patients, I often offer the comment, "I will not use a tongue depressor so you can relax and open your mouth widely without fear of gagging." Aggressive use of tongue blades can even induce choking and vomiting.

Children, in particular, do not tend to do well with tongue blades. Many children have been so victimized by tongue depressors that even a seasoned physician cannot examine them. I have had many frightened children refuse to open their mouths for an exam no matter what methods I used to persuade them. These situations are generally avoidable if children are properly handled by health professionals early on.

Reassurance and patience will often help children overcome their fears. Parents may want to work with their children before the exam. Practice with your child at home in a non-threatening environment, first opening your mouth and then having your child peer in. Then ask them to do the same. With this kind of practice, they will become use to throat and mouth exams. During your office visit, ask that a tongue depressor not be used if your child is fearful of it or is prone to gagging.

Under most circumstances, it is unnecessary to use a tongue depressor when obtaining a throat culture. A simple cotton-tipped applicator applied to a well-opened throat is less obtrusive and more effective. Tongue depressors should be used as a last resort.

Chapter 47

Throat Cultures or Quick Strep Tests?

Approximately 19% of all upper respiratory tract infections are due to strep throat. This illness varies in frequency during the year and occurs more commonly during the winter and spring. As most parents know, strep is most frequently seen in school age children. Infected children often spread the disease to friends and siblings through direct or close contact from tiny respiratory droplets that harbor the bacteria. Contaminated food, especially milk products, as well as glasses or other containers can also result in outbreaks.

Typical symptoms of strep throat include a red sore throat, sometimes accompanied by white patches on the tonsils. Some patients will have swollen neck glands, headache, abdominal pain and fever, while others may have just a sore throat. The incubation period, referring to the duration of time from exposure until the onset of symptoms, is typically two to four days. Untreated patients remain contagious for up to three weeks, whereas treated patients are no longer infectious within two to four days after starting their medicine.

Tests to detect Group A beta-hemolytic streptococcus are commonly performed in physicians' offices. Patients experiencing the recent onset of a sore throat may be asked to provide a specimen to detect strep by using a rapid or quick test method. This test checks for the presence of a unique antigen or by-product of the strep bacteria that infects a sick patient's throat. This antigen can be found both in acutely ill patients and in patients who appear well, but may be carriers of the bacteria.

Antigens can remain in the back of your throat for up to two months and may result in a positive quick strep test even when you have been cured. If you experience another sore throat soon after finishing a course of antibiotics, you may need to undergo another throat culture. A properly-obtained culture will identify the actual strep bacteria. After one has been cured, a repeat throat culture may read negative, meaning no strep organisms were identified. If your antibiotic fails to work, due to a resistant form of strep, then your throat culture would remain positive, meaning the bacteria is still found in your throat. A quick strep test may remain positive for weeks after successful therapy has been completed and therefore is not a satisfactory method to determine if a cure has occurred.

Treatment of strep throat will reduce symptoms, decrease the spread of the disease and will reduce complications such as rheumatic fever, scarlet fever, and glomerulonephritis. If left untreated, these diseases may cause permanent damage to one's heart or kidneys.

The usual treatment for strep throat includes penicillin or erythromycin in penicillin-allergic patients. Increasing resistance to erythromycin with failure rates as high as 25% has been seen. Fortunately, other effective antibiotics are available. After being on an effective antibiotic for a few days, patients will rapidly improve and may be tempted to quit their antibiotics prematurely. Less than ten days worth of therapy may prove ineffective; except in the case of Vantin – a drug approved recently by the FDA for a five-day course of treatment. Failure to complete a full course of treatment as recommended by your physician increases your chances of becoming a carrier or suffering the complications of heart or kidney disease.

If one family member is being treated for strep throat, it may also be wise to screen other household members who appear well, but may carry the strep organisms in their throat simply from being exposed. Strep carriers often do not experience sore throat or other symptoms, but they nevertheless may infect others. All patients who have been infected with strep must be treated until a negative throat culture has been achieved. A follow up throat culture should be obtained about four days after completing a full course of antibiotics to verify a cure. If your doctor has not recommended a throat culture after you have finished a course of antibiotics, be sure and request one.

Inadequately treated strep is potentially as serious as untreated strep. A quick strep test cannot be used after treatment to determine a cure. Should you or your child develop another suspicious throat infection within two months of a previous strep infection, a quick strep test should not be used for diagnostic purposes. A twenty-four hour throat culture is the most reliable test to look for reinfection within a one to two month time frame.

Chapter 48

Blood Drawing: How to Make it Easier

Although many modern tests require blood specimens, most people dislike being stuck with needles and will go to almost any length to avoid this procedure. Typically, however, only minimal pain will occur from blood drawing if you follow the lab technician's instructions.

Holding still and then making a fist after a tourniquet has been applied will help the vein to enlarge or dilate for easy location. Holding still is extremely important. Moving after the needle has pierced the vein may cause the needle to further damage your vein or cause unnecessary pain if the needle tip brushes up against the wall of your vein. Sitting or lying perfectly still will ease the collection of blood and minimize one's discomfort.

After the needle has been removed from your vein, a cotton ball will be applied to the site of needle entry. Direct pressure over the area with cotton and a finger or two will help suppress bleeding. Direct pressure accompanied by arm elevation above one's heart for sixty seconds will further reduce the chance of bleeding. This technique should eliminate the chance of a blood blister or bruise forming at the site of needle entry and will also prevent your clothes from being soiled with blood once pressure has been released.

Some patients are prone to lightheadedness or fainting during or after their blood has been drawn. If you are prone to feeling lightheaded or dizzy during any uncomfortable exam or test, please let your health care provider know this in advance. They will then be prepared to reposition you into a lying position should the need occur; thereby, avoiding a fall or possible head trauma during a procedure.

A device now available can be used to reduce a child's pain from a needle stick. It is a system called "Numby Stuff" manufactured by IOMED, Salt Lake City, Utah. The equipment through a process referred to as iontophoresis transfers an anesthetic into the skin over a vein. The child can assist the process by turning a knob on the device. When correctly applied several minutes before the needle stick has occurred, the device will deliver pain relieving anesthetic into the skin. "Numby Stuff" can cause a tingling sensation in some children somewhat like a pins and needles sensation. For children requiring repeated visits to labs for blood drawing, requesting that this inexpensive device be purchased by your lab for use may be a worthwhile consideration.

Chapter 49

Immunizations: A Forgotten Blessing

"Vaccines are one of the most far-reaching and effective technologies of our time."
-- **Bill Gates**, after donating $25 million dollars to the International AIDS Vaccine Initiative

In August of 1998 near the North Pole, a group of scientists wearing biohazard suits dug into a mass grave of six coal miners who had perished from the Spanish Influenza epidemic of 1918. These scientists hoped to find traces of the virus that had killed 21 million victims worldwide, since determining its genetic makeup might help with the development of new and better vaccines. This and other research is needed to discover new vaccines to fight a growing army of hazardous bacteria and viruses. Vaccines will be our main defense against this enemy of resistant microbes.

Immunization is the process of protecting humans and animals from infectious diseases through the use of vaccines. Vaccines are composed of substances that the body reacts to by forming antibodies to the foreign substance. Vaccines are usually injected into the deltoid muscle of the upper arm when administered to an adult or child. In an infant injections are often placed into the thigh muscles. Once exposed to an effective vaccine, the body's defense mechanisms will form new antibodies to fight off the infection when later exposed to it. Activating the body's defenses prevents the disease from developing. Therefore no symptoms would become apparent once you have been properly immunized. Some vaccines provide life-long immunity, while others must be repeated every few years.

223

Immunizations to prevent disease remain underutilized. Part of the problem is that too much time, money and effort is being spent on acute care, and not enough attention is being placed on preventive health care. Patients sometimes choose not to participate in preventive medicine, and physicians themselves sometimes do not place enough emphasis on the benefits of immunization. Time constraints in the practice of medicine can be a physician's greatest enemy, and discussions about preventive medicine often take a back seat to treating acute illnesses.

I believe that federal and state governments should play a larger role in educating patients about proper immunizations. They should assist in providing opportunities to receive free immunizations as they did in the 1950s, when polio vaccines were distributed nationwide – an approach which has totally eliminated the occurrence of natural polio in our country.

Many middle-aged and older adults remember the vaccination they first had as a child that left a dime-sized scar on their upper outer arm. This was the small pox vaccination, given universally in a campaign that lasted decades. It proved exceptionally effective, completely eliminating a disease that had threatened mankind for ages. The last recorded case of naturally occurring small pox occurred in Somalia in October of 1977. Because small pox was the first and to date the only disease totally eliminated on earth, the vaccine is no longer needed.

The obvious success of the worldwide small pox campaign should provide incentive for dealing with other dangerous infectious diseases such as Hepatitis B, measles, rubella, polio and the current most dreaded example, AIDS. Although there are vaccines available to combat a variety of viruses, there are none yet developed which protect against AIDS – though scientists are working on it.

Many patients refuse vaccinations, due to fear associated with needle pain or post-injection muscle pain. They believe the resultant pain after the injection will limit their activities. Some worry about developing post injection flu-like symptoms a few days later. Most current immunizations result in minimal muscle pain and few if any side effects. Those that occur tend to be short-lived should they happen at all. Tetanus shots and the tetanus diptheria vaccine are the most notorious in causing soreness, redness and swelling of one's arm after injection. Fortunately, these adverse side effects occur in only twenty-five percent of patients receiving injections. Within two to four days, their arm is generally fine, and their newfound immunity will last for eight to ten years.

An anesthetic cream or patch known as EMLA (Eutectic Mixture of Local Anesthetic) is available for local use prior to an injection to reduce or eliminate pain. To be effective, it must be placed over the injection sight one hour before the vaccine is used. In most cases it will also reduce post injection pain and should be considered for use in patients with a past history of this problem.

A dose of naproxen sodium administered thirty to sixty minutes prior to a diphtheria tetanus injection can help relieve muscle pain as well. In my experience over the years in using naproxen for this purpose, most patients did not develop arm pain after being given the vaccine. For best results, a patient could take a medicine such as naproxen or ibuprophen one half-hour to one hour before leaving home if they are scheduled to receive a vaccine. Most vaccines, such as the flu or pneumococcal vaccine, cause less painful reactions and do not require the use of an anti-inflammatory medication. This practice also would not apply to children, who actually tend to complain less about vaccines than do adults. Those of you who are allergic to ibuprofen and similar medications or have a history of stomach disorders and other contraindications to their use should not use these medications without consulting your physician.

So if you are known to suffer significant post-injection pain, suggest to your physician three possible alternatives. First, request that an anti-inflammatory drug such as naproxen be administered orally before or soon after the injection. Secondly, ask that a small-bore needle be used to minimize initial surface pain. And thirdly, ask that the injection be administered *slowly*, after the needle has been advanced. Rapid injection of any substance into muscle will result in unnecessary trauma to the

225

muscle. Some patients may wish to take a second dose of naproxen twelve hours later when at home but usually this step is unnecessary. Also, vaccines should not be administered if you or your child are sick with even a low-grade fever.

There are a few ideas that can be tried in infants to reduce pain prior to an immunization. According to Dr. William Zempsky, assistant professor of pediatrics at the University of Connecticut School of Medicine, studies have shown that skin to skin contact between a mother and her child will decrease pain at the time of an immunization. Therefore cheek to cheek contact may be helpful in these situations. Also a pacifier placed in your infants mouth will reduce pain especially if it's been coated with sugar immediately prior to the child's injection.

After you have been given a vaccine, wait until you feel comfortable and not lightheaded before leaving your physician's office. In rare instances, some patients may suffer an allergic reaction to a vaccine and will require immediate treatment. Most serious reactions occur within a few minutes if they are to occur at all. Some patients exhibit lightheadedness from any injection and will be asked to lie down for a few minutes while an assistant elevates their legs above heart level. This technique will provide extra blood flow to the brain, eliminating lightheadedness in seconds. Even for those who feel fine, waiting for ten minutes in the exam or waiting room before leaving will provide additional security should an adverse reaction occur. The sore arm syndrome will show up later, if at all, and can be treated at home with ibuprofen should you experience this problem. In my office experience, I have never known of a patient to suffer an allergic reaction or a serious side effect to any vaccine I have administered, though the possibility always exists.

Vaccines occasionally are associated with unexpected complications once they are placed into widespread use. In 1999, a new vaccine was widely used to prevent rotovirus infections, the leading cause of childhood diarrhea. It was taken off the market when unexpected problems occurred.

Another vaccine has recently been released to prevent Lyme Disease and should be used by those of you who live in areas or will travel to areas where Lyme Disease is prevalent. Soon an influenza vaccine that can be taken nasally with fewer side effects than flu shots will be available. In the near future a new pneumococcal vaccine will be available for use in children to reduce the frequency of several forms of upper respiratory tract bacterial infections that now cause many childhood problems.

One last point is worth noting. Children or adults with weakened immune systems due to diseases such as AIDS or those undergoing chemotherapy should not be given live virus vaccines.

Chapter 50

Ouch!: The Painful Ear

One of the most common reasons for seeing a pediatrician or a family physician is to treat swimmer's ear, referred to in medical terminology as external otitis. This is an infection of the ear canal resulting in swelling, redness and prominent pain.

The ear, infected or not, is a tender part of the anatomy that is often painful to examine. When examining the ear, it's often necessary to pull backward and upward on the outer ear to straighten out the naturally curved ear canal in order to visualize the entire ear drum. This maneuver can cause exquisite pain when the ear canal is already uncomfortable from infection. Alert your physician if your ear is tender so that he will use extra care in his examination. Sometimes busy physicians can be hasty during an examination, causing more pain then necessary. We do not wish to hurt patients, but sometimes routine care makes us forget about patients' needs and feelings so a little reminder now and then is graciously accepted.

Chapter 51

The Pelvic and Rectal Exam: I Don't Think So!!

Another exam which many women dread is the pelvic exam. All but the most jaded physicians recognize this problem, yet no reasonable alternative has yet been devised. However, all is not lost. If you have a terrible problem with a pelvic exam, first prepare yourself mentally in an appropriate manner. It is important to recognize that most of the discomfort is avoidable by various relaxation techniques. Fear or embarrassment in many patients causes their vaginal and perineal muscles to tighten up so vigorously that introducing even one or two fingers into the vaginal canal can prove uncomfortable.

If one is relaxed and mentally prepared, the exam should be nearly pain-free, unless one is experiencing a pelvic infection. Even then, when done properly, minimal pain need be induced. Be sure to ask your doctor to warm and lubricate the vaginal speculum with warm water before insertion. It's simple to do and appreciated by most. Next, remain calm and ask your physician to please be gentle. Pushing, prodding and squeezing vigorously in this tender area of the body is not necessary. Letting your doctor know of your concerns in advance should reduce your anxiety and discomfort.

Another exam that causes some patients discomfort is the rectal exam. In my experience, men are more repulsed than women at the thought of this invasion. In fact, many become lightheaded during the exam and may even pass out. If from past experience this has been a problem, mention your concerns to your doctor. The exam can then be done while lying on your side on an exam table rather than bending over the end of an exam table, which can possibly result in a blackout and a fall to the floor.

The rectum is another sensitive area that should be examined with care and respect. You should not hesitate in asking your doctor to be as gentle as possible during the exam. When a well-lubricated and gloved finger is slowly admitted into the rectum,

231

you will feel minimal if any pain. The key word here is *slowly*.
Playing an active role in your examination will reduce fear and
provide control and security.

Chapter 52

Outside Labs and X-Ray Facilities

After your exam, your doctor may have to send you to another medical facility or specialist. Before you leave your physician's office, be sure you have the proper lab slips, x-ray slip or referral slip in hand, since most tests cannot be carried out without a physician's orders. You must also remember that most expensive tests such as CAT scans or MRIs need pre-approval from your health insurance carrier. If these expensive tests are not pre-approved they often will not be covered, resulting in stress, aggravation and extra expense. Generally, you should assume that you will have to pay for any specialized tests or referrals that have not been properly approved in advance by your insurance company. Costly errors can be eliminated if you are prepared to work with your physician's office staff to ensure proper approval. Just as importantly, be sure tests are conducted in a hospital or other facility approved by your insurance company. As the beneficiary of your health insurance plan, you must be completely familiar with the established rules pertaining to laboratory testing, physician referrals and hospital visits.

SECTION VI: MISCELLANEOUS ISSUES AND CONCERNS

Chapter 53

Communication and Intimacy in Primary Care

A number of problems that continually surface in the delivery of medical care can lead to disruption of the doctor-patient relationship. The first and most important area of concern is that of communication. A patient of mine, Richard Burrows, said to me some time ago, "You have to be able to communicate with your doctor."

To communicate is to transmit some form of information from one person or group to that of another. However, the message must not only be received, but it also must be understood. Too often, patients have a conversation with their physician about difficult and confusing problems, often resulting in misunderstandings or confusion. Linda Greider in an article, Talking Back to Your Doctor Works, *AARP Bulletin*, February 2000, commented that research indicates physicians will listen only twenty-three seconds to a patient's initial comments about their problem before interrupting to ask questions or change the subject. This practice sounds quite rude, nor was the reason revealed possibly because it may not have been studied. I speculate among other things, it may relate to a physician's limited time in today's medical office environment. The point here is to be well prepared from the onset to state exactly what your primary problem or medical concern is. Sometimes your physician may not fully understand what you are thinking or worrying about especially when your health concerns may involve sensitive areas or marital problems. The office visit belongs to you, but failure to successfully explain your problem may result in a wasted visit. It is equally possible that you may not understand what your doctor is attempting to communicate to you after he has evaluated you. Neither situation is ideal.

If you believe that your physician is not truly grasping your problem, do not hesitate to say, "Doctor, I just do not think you understand my problem. Let's start over." If after explaining your concerns to your physician you remain uncomfortable or dissatisfied, it is important that you make your concerns apparent to him. Since you have taken the time and effort to see your doctor, you deserve (to the degree that your problem has been evaluated) a clear explanation of what your diagnosis and treatment is. Patients have a strong desire for knowledge. In an article that appeared in August, 1998, in the journal, *Hippocrates*, Dr. Leo Galland remarked that partients "have an intense need for an explanation of the cause of their illness, but doctors are usually content to name a disease and treat it.... Information can reduce anxiety, increase feelings of control, encourage healthier behaviors, and improve the ability to cope with pain." Should your physician not provide the answers you crave, ask that he spend a minute or so to explain to your satisfaction. Doctors tend to underestimate the time they spend in patient education. We also have a tendency to believe patients understand illnesses better than they do.

Even when the exact cause of your problem is not well understood by your physician, he/she can often put your mind at ease to some degree. Many patients come to see physicians with the fear of cancer or some other serious problem in the back of their mind. More often than not, their fears are unfounded. Usually your doctor can provide some degree of comfort once you have expressed to him or her what exactly worries you.

Sometimes your symptoms will warrant careful analysis. Persistent pain without an obvious explanation deserves your physician's complete attention. If you do not feel satisfied with your doctor's answers after his evaluation, it is important to make your position perfectly clear in a pleasant way. Never leave your physician's office bearing the burden of unfinished business. If you remain uncomfortable, request a follow-up visit or an opinion from other experts.

Another major area of concern in the modern practice of medicine involves the cost of providing medical care. If you have major financial concerns, it is important for you to let your doctor be aware of them. Doctors can be flexible in selecting certain tests and prescribing certain drugs, and it is better for a patient to have an affordable medication that may not be state-of-the-art than to have no medication at all. Prescriptions for expensive medications that go unfilled will provide no relief or benefit. Voicing your financial concerns to your physician may allow him to find other avenues that are effective in providing care at a lower cost.

Intimacy and trust are the basis of a sound doctor-patient relationship; it is important that both patient and physician understand each other's feelings. Without understanding the full impact of a problem on a patient's life, it may not be possible for a physician to understand all of the consequences either. Thus a patient must provide, when necessary, all relevant details. Not to do so can be misleading.

To receive the best care, you must be careful to choose a competant physician. Good communication will get you nowhere if your doctor is less skilled or conscientious than he or she should be. When looking for a physician, look both for caring qualities and for competence. I have seen many patients treated by kind and gentle physicians who fail to keep up with new trends in preventive medicine or state-of-the-art medical science. As a result, many of these patients languished in a state of mediocre health, even teetering on the edge of disaster. In some cases, a patient's blood pressure was always just a little too high, or their colon polyps were never found. The mammogram was never suggested. The smoking habit was overlooked as being too challenging. The drinking problem was never noticed. The seat belts were never discussed. The ball was simply dropped time and time again.

In 1998 an estimated 564,800 Americans died from cancer; 43,900 from breast cancer, 56,500 from rectal and colon cancer, 39,200 from prostatic cancer and 4,900 from cervical cancer. According to *The Journal of the American Board of Family Practice*, January-February, 2000, these deaths were potentially avoidable through early detection via careful screening. The article indicates that the percentages of eligible women who have been screened for breast cancer (28%) and cervical cancer (52%) in the past two years is unacceptably low and below the standards set by *Healthy People* 2000. Your single best chance of receiving careful screening is through awareness and by participation in regular health maintenance visits as listed in the appendix.

Our health is not a question of luck, but more often a question of choices and knowledge. Knowing what to do, what to look for and then doing it will usually result in a long and reasonably pleasant life. If you follow the precepts of sound preventive medicine, you can usually overcome "bad luck." Bad luck, however, is simply making bad choices and not learning what is required for good health.

Chapter 54

The Telephone Jungle

During the first two hours of the morning or afternoon session, a patient may have difficulty in getting through to their physician's office. Should you be inquiring about a routine appointment, it is best to call in late morning or late afternoon to improve your odds of penetrating the telephone jungle. If you have an urgent problem, waiting to call later may not be wise. Calling early would still be your best choice, though you may become involved in a telephone traffic jam.

In busy offices, the phone rarely rests, resulting in flustered office personnel who may become short or rude. A rude front office staff is never acceptable and is sometimes a reason for patients to leave an otherwise excellent physician. Physicians are rarely aware of conversations between patients and office staff. If you feel you've been mistreated, a letter to your doctor with the name of the unhelpful employee may resolve many problems for you and for others. Communication is vitally important. Quality and service improve if enough people make their views heard. A letter to your HMO may also go a long way in resolving problems should your needs go unheeded at your physicians office, since contractual agreements between physician's and HMOs require convenient office hours, proper urgent care support, after-hours backup call, and high-quality medical care.

Primary care physicians need to develop new ways of increasing patient satisfaction through new technologies. Karen Ignagni, chief executive officer of American Association of Health Plans Washington, suggests improving patient communication by using e-mail. Being more efficient and generally less time consuming, e-mail could in many situations replace the telephone for scheduling appointments. It could also be used to forward laboratory results and even answer patient's questions and concerns. Physicians are somewhat slower in accepting newer business technologies, but as patients you are in a position to encourage their use through constructive suggestions to your physicians of choice.

Chapter 55

Medical Records: Ownership and Secrets Revealed

Patients regularly have questions about who has access to their medical records. Regulations controlling access vary from state to state and are somewhat diverse. In general, however, your medical record is the property of your physician. It remains a confidential record, and its contents are protected under the law. You are the only one besides your physician who is entitled to the information in your record, unless a court orders differently. Unfortunately there is a growing body of evidence indicating that other entities such as insurers, managed care organizations and pharmacies may have access to medical records, according to Paul S. Appelbaum, MD, as noted in JAMA, February 9, 2000. "Although 40% of respondents to a 1998 survey believed that the privacy of their medical records was protected by federal law, in fact no comprehensive federal legislation or regulation exists."

There are times when you will want others to have access to your medical records. You may occasionally wish to have specific physicians you have selected review your record. This can become necessary when more than one physician is involved in your care, or if you change doctors. As a courtesy, copies of medical records are usually sent free of charge to consulting physicians or new primary care physicians upon your request and with written permission. Some patients wish to have a copy of their medical record. A copy can be made available to you if you request it, though a fee to defray the cost of labor, equipment, and materials will probably be assessed.

Becoming familiar with the contents of your medical record is important if you are to understand your overall health. Your medical record is composed of progress notes pertaining to each office visit, physical examination forms of various types, consultant's letters, immunization records, laboratory results, x-rays, specialized scans, pathology reports, medication lists, flow sheets and a variety of other important reference materials. It is worthwhile for you to be familiar with this information.

Because you have been the subject of each office visit, reviewing progress notes or physical exam findings in your record are not essential. Simply jotting down a few sentences in a notebook about your visit upon its conclusion will serve you well. You must also be aware of completed test results, including blood tests, x-rays, mammograms, ultrasound studies, C.T. scans and M.R.I's. Physicians have traditionally shielded their patients from this information, incorrectly believing that patients cannot handle it. In fact, many patients are so well informed – with access to the internet, television, and magazines – that they are comfortable discussing or researching many of their own health concerns. With that in mind, copies of your laboratory findings should be made available to you upon request. In fact, it would not be too much of a stretch for testing facilities to routinely send a copy of all lab and x-ray data to you as well as to your physician. If you had copies of your test results, problems associated with lost or misfiled forms in your medical record would be reduced. Yes, some of the information may be alarming or difficult to understand. You may want to review the findings with your physician at your next office appointment. If you still remain alarmed by an unexpected test result, most physicians will accept a phone call or arrange for a brief visit to explain the test results and hopefully put your mind at ease.

Before lab or x-ray slips and similar forms are placed in your medical record, your physician will initial or sign the reports indicating he has seen them. Due to large volumes of materials being placed in medical records on a daily basis, however, a lab slip or report of some kind may have been placed in your record without your physician's knowledge. This scenario is uncommon, but it does happen on occasion. As mentioned above, reviewing copies of your test results reduces the likelihood of an abnormal test (such as a suspicious mammogram) going by unnoticed. Even if you do not have access to a copy of your test results you must be sure and check

244

with your physician's office on all matters of testing. If a test is worth doing, it's worth knowing about.

Taking an active role in understanding the contents of your medical record is a must. Assembling your own medical record for home use – including personalized notes, lab reports and consultant's reports – will serve you well. Yes, even acquiring consultant's reports are helpful. What did your cardiologist or neurologist say to you about your last visit? Many patients simply do not remember. You may want to have access to this information eventually for several reasons including when traveling or when changing physicians. Transfer of medical records are often not achieved in a timely fashion.

In summary, be sure and check on all test results one way or the other. Take an active role in understanding most of your medical record. Remaining an alert and involved partner in your health care will serve you well. As physicians, we want you to receive comprehensive care. You can help us deliver it.

Review of Medical Records by Insurance Companies

Medical insurance companies will often review your record prior to granting new or extended medical coverage. When insurance companies request information, your physician will require a signed release form from you before copies of your record can be forwarded. Life insurance companies, as well, may request copies of medical records before adding or extending coverage. Without your permission, however, copies of records cannot be released.

When you change your medical insurance coverage, your new insurance company may request copies of old records to evaluate pre-existing medical conditions, which may not be covered. However, many medical insurance companies, especially those who extend coverage to Medicare patients, provide fairly comprehensive coverage through their HMO contracts without regard to pre-existing conditions. Before switching insurance companies, try to determine when and if a pre-existing medical problem is covered or will alter your benefits. Usually, after being with a new insurance company for

245

between ninety days and a year, pre-existing conditions are covered. Legislation may eventually require that insurance companies provide coverage for pre-existing conditions, whether or not you were covered previously.

Chapter 56

Fear of the Unknown

It is surprising how many individuals – generally men and the elderly – fail to receive timely medical care. Women are the primary force in providing for medical care for themselves and for their families. They are the ones who generally prod the rest of us into action. Unfortunately, prodding doesn't always work. Many patients claim to feel fine, have no medical symptoms, brag about never seeing a doctor and basically bury their heads in the sand when it comes to routine health care checkups.

They believe that if nothing is bothering them, then nothing is wrong. This is largely true of younger adults. It turns out that if the average young adult was to wear seat belts, avoid street drugs, avoid dangerous areas and practice safe sex, most would pass through the first four decades of life apparently unscathed. The word "apparently" is important. Here is wherein the problem lies. Our bodies have such a large amount of built-in reserve capacity that serious underlying damage may be occurring even when we are unaware of it. Smoking, drinking, poor eating habits, lack of exercise, genetics and simply aging are all taking their toll, even when we aren't aware of it. Then, in the fifth or sixth decade of life, we're in the hospital or battling some unforeseen enemy.

Patients often later say, "How could this happen so suddenly?" The fact is, it didn't happen suddenly. There is rarely any disease that occurs without warning, short of a bursting brain aneurysm. Unbeknownst to us, most conditions have been evolving over many years. Through negligence or bad habits, we systematically ruin our bodies, but we just don't realize that anything is going on. Some of us actually realize the consequences of bad habits, but we may not want to admit them to ourselves. Since we are probably feeling fine, we fail to seek routine preventive health care. Some women, for example, fail to perform a self-breast examination on a monthly basis. Some fifty-year-old men fail to have annual prostate exams to detect early cancer.

Many patients fail to seek medical care because they fear the possibility that cancer may be discovered. My answer to them is, let's find it if it's there. Caught early enough, most cancers are curable. If you are harboring cancer and it is not found early enough, your days may be numbered. Finding it in its early stages may save your life.

Not seeing a physician regularly is not going to prevent an existing cancer, as some people seem to think. "I've been lucky so far. Why change my luck?" they say. Good health, however, is not a question of luck. You must make your own luck by practicing preventive medicine and seeking routine health care, even if it means paying for some of the costs yourself. *Let's get lucky.* See your doctor, find out where you stand, and receive proper direction on all health related issues.

Another group of people who fail to see physicians are those who have experienced previously bad results with the health care system or retain bad memories of problems experienced by friends or relatives.

Negative feelings are understandable, but you must overcome them for the sake of your own health. Good medical care is complicated and difficult, but the effort is worthwhile. "Practice makes perfect," and like physicians, many patients won't get it right the first time. Awareness, effort and perseverance will eventually pay off with good or improved health.

Chapter 57

Will You Help Teaching Institutions Teach?

As long as there are physicians, there will be medical students and residents in training, learning the science and art of medicine. Since no two patients are alike, there will always be a need for ongoing education by hands-on examination. Reading about medical problems, no matter the depth and detail of the material available, can never adequately replace hands-on medicine. As physicians, we must learn by doing, listening and touching. Many of the finest physicians will gravitate towards institutions of higher learning, hoping to pass on their expertise to others, thereby fulfilling a requirement of the Hippocratic Oath. Likewise, many patients with complex or poorly understood medical problems also frequent these institutions when the need occurs.

At teaching centers such as The Cleveland Clinic Foundation, patients will often first be evaluated by a medical student or resident in training, sometimes referred to as a fellow. On the surface, additional examinations appear to some patients as a waste of time or an invasion of privacy. But please remember, each and every physician without exception learned initially through the gracious participation of countless patients, who then later repeated the same process with a fully-certified physician or specialist. Without this *voluntary* participation by patients, physicians would be unable to learn the art and practice of medicine.

Chapter 58

Getting Your Doctor's Attention

A few patients do not return to their previous physician because they feel their doctor didn't care, didn't listen, talked above their head, or may simply have been incompetent. Most physicians are competent, but they lack appropriate communication skills or a good bedside manner. Patients, for any number of reasons, can be turned off by a physician, his office staff or his office policies. This can run the gamut from being rudely treated to not being treated at all. Most physicians wish to provide "world class care."

All too often, problems may arise that are not brought to the attention of a physician. Over the years, I have happily received many letters of thanks, but occasionally a few letters have been sent that were critical. I have made the mistake of saving the complimentary letters that were *good for my ego* while casting away the unfavorable ones that were *good for my practice*. These disparaging letters have done more for improving how I practice and deliver health care than other sources of enlightenment.

Early on in my career, I was resentful of uncomplimentary comments, but I have learned to use them to improve my practice skills and office management techniques. I remember early in the 1980's as a young private practitioner, a mother once wrote to me complaining that I had not talked to her children during their recent office visit but instead had only questioned her about their symptoms. She felt this could lead to a lack of trust on the part of her children or even worse, an incorrect diagnosis. With that, she wrote she would be seeking medical care elsewhere. I was awakened by this letter, resulting in completely changing my methods in dealing with children. I learned that talking with even very young children was a valuable part of the doctor-patient relationship. Overtime children became less fearful of their visits and also more cooperative. In fact many children look forward to seeing me

251

because we often have fun together. That particular letter from a concerned mother changed how I dealt with children forever.

Should you feel uncomfortable with any issue about your health care, call or write your physician and discuss your concerns. If your physician is open-minded as should be the case, progress is often made and a stronger doctor-patient relationshop will result. It's been my experience that usually patients complain out of fear of the unknown, fear that something will be overlooked or some service will not be provided in a respectful or timely fashion.

Physicians who do not recognize the existence of a problem cannot correct it. Awareness of a problem by your doctor is more than half the battle. Help your doctor to improve how he practices medicine through thoughtful communication with his patients. When necessary, appropriate letter writing will eventually have a positive effect in some fashion though at first it may not appear to do so. Some physicians who are strongly offended may dismiss a patient from their practice but this would be an exceptional result. Few of us would want to be treated by an arrogant or uncaring physician anyway. Most of us wish to be treated by empathetic physicians interested as much in helping us as they are in treating us.

The lesson to be learned is this: a well-written letter to your physician outlining your problem or concern can help both of you.

Should your physician not be sensitve enough to your needs, consider enclosing a copy of Sir Osler's thoughts along with your letter.

The following quote written in 1899, by Sir William Osler, considered to be the father of modern medicine, was given to me years ago during my training. The source to me is unknown so I will be unable to provide credit. It is a thought provoking paragraph that most physicians would do well by heeding.

"Be careful when you get into practice to cultivate equally well your hearts and your heads. There is a

252

strong feeling abroad among people that we doctors are given over nowadays to science...we care much more for the disease and the scientific aspects of it than for the individual. I would urge upon you to care more particularly for the individual patient than for the special features of the disease. Dealing as we do with poor, suffering humanity, we see the man unmasked or, so to speak, exposed to all the frailities and weaknesses. You have to keep your heart pretty soft and pretty tender not to get too great a contemp for your fellow creatures. The best way to do that is to keep a looking-glass in your hearts, and the more carefully you scan your own frailities, the more tender you are for the frailities of your fellow creatures."

Chapter 59

What You Must Know About What Your Doctor Must Know

Many of us have a great deal of interest in our general health and well being. On a daily basis, we read or hear about new breakthroughs in the field of medical science, and we wonder how this new knowledge may apply to us. Many of you are aware of the importance of preventive medicine and early disease detection. Unfortunately many patients ignore this important aspect of their health care. On the other hand, these same individuals take a keen interest in proper maintenance of their automobile or SUV. Based on a study I did years ago, I learned that most people spend a great deal more money on routine automobile maintenance than they do on routine health maintenance. On average, however, routine physical exams, immunizations, and basic lab studies are less expensive than automobile maintenance.

Many of you may wonder why health insurance plans do not always cover routine physical exams and basic lab tests (I use the term health insurance loosely since some plans do not encourage us to maintain good health since they don't provide for it). Some insurance companies claim that studies show the overall cost of performing routine lab studies on all of their enrollees would cost more money than the amount required to treat certain diseases in a small percentage of patients. For example, the cost of performing annual chest x-rays in all asymptomatic smokers (those without symptoms) to look for early lung cancer would probably cost more than treating lung cancer found in patients after they develop symptoms. Of course finding lung cancer in symptomatic patients may prove to be too late to insure a cure.

Some experts believe that physicians are primarily accountable for providing for all patient needs. In *Family Practice Management*, January 2000, Marc L. Rivo, MD, MPH, stated, "In the new century, we (physicians) will find ourselves accountable not just for the care we deliver but also for the care we don't deliver." For example, should your physician fail to diagnose an early cancer by forgetting to recommend available screening tests universally recommended by medical authorities you may have a case for litigation. This may be true, but I am not convinced of the wisdom of placing full responsibility in the hands of your physician as the practice of medicine grows more complicated. Once the damage is done, resorting to litigation may result in financial remuneration but it will not restore you to normal health. Sooner or later mistakes though unintentional, will affect many of you. As the captain of your ship, you have a personal responsibility to assist in your own health care in order to reduce the chance of errors of omission.

Comprehensive preventive health and screening is a necessity for all patients who hope to lead a longer and healthier life. In many medical offices, not enough is being done due to time constraints. A study by Kimberly S, H. Yarnell, MD, and Barbara K. Rimer, DrPh, reported in *The Journal of the American Board of Family Practice* noted, "our study findings suggest that a major barrier to physicians performing screening is lack of time during the encounter, which is not surprising, as most primary care physicians must address both the patient's agenda and presenting complaints and screening in an average 10-15 minute visit." In their study, they tracked the compliance levels of physicians using a computerized system to aid in screening patients for recommended health maintenance. Their results were less then hoped for even when using "state of-the-art prompting devices." According to the study, doctors used the devices only 50 percent of the time and completed health maintenance needs in less than 50 percent of the office visits. The study indicated that part of the problem is related to "increasing stresses on primary care clinicians to provide more management of all patient's medical needs...."

As the main beneficiary, patients must take responsibility for insuring that you and your family receive the health care that you deserve. Specific recommendations for preventive medicine and services are not obvious to the average patient and continually evolve as time and medical science advance. Learn what you must about current preventive health concepts. Between various health organizations and medical specialties, there may be slightly different schedules. Should conflicts occur, always follow the recommendations of your family physician or primary care specialist.

See Appendix C at the end of the book for recommendations which have been assembled and are based on the current medical thinking of many medical organizations. Each year, new recommendations will be proposed, and therefore this list will remain in a constant state of flux. Following current recommendations will provide a good basis for your health at least for the next few years until theories change. Later editions will keep you abreast of recommendations in the field of preventive health care and maintenance. The secret to long life is to keep people out of trouble, not to bale them out.

Chapter 60

The Final Chapter Is Yours to Write

The final chapter of this book is the beginning of a new way for you to work with your physician, other health care personnel, and the health care system. By following the suggestions in this book, you will be able to take charge of your health care. Becoming a partner in your health care requires responsibility, personal involvement, follow-through, and ongoing participation. The best physicians read and study current medical journals and attend continuing medical education forums. Like them, you must keep abreast of your health problems, remain aware of preventive medicine practices, and consider new innovations in health care. We all can improve our health if we remain devoted to the best that medical science has to offer. We can achieve the best by demanding the best. Knowing and not doing is equivalent to not knowing at all. Take advantage of your newfound knowledge each and every day.

Sit down and think about how you will relate and participate during your medical evaluation. Arrive prepared with the facts about your symptoms, an up-to-date list of medications, an account of past surgeries, a summary of chronic medical problems, and a current medical insurance manual. To know where you are going, you need to know where you have been. There is very little luck involved with achieving good health.

The luckiest patients I know are well-prepared for their visit, practice the best preventive medicine principles, and remain steadfast in their goals of leading a long and healthy life.

On the profession of medicine Lord Bryce once called medicine "the only profession that labors incessantly to destroy the reason for its own existence." *We need your help*!!

"It should be the function of medicine to have people die young as late as possible."
Ernst L. Wynder

259

APPENDICES

APPENDIX A

The purpose of this form is to enable parents to authorize treatment for minor children who become ill or injured when parents are unable to accompany the child to the office, or in emergency situations when a parent is unable to be reached.

PERMISSION FOR TREATMENT OF A MINOR

In the event that reasonable attempts to contact me at _____ (home phone) _____ (work phone)_____ or (cell phone) have been unsuccessful, I hereby authorize _____or _____ or a physician appointed by either of these persons in my absence to treat my child (or children), _____ , a minor(s), on an emergency basis in my absence.

I, the undersigned, consent to any necessary x-ray examination, laboratory examination, anesthetic and medical or surgical diagnosis or treatment which is deemed advisable for my child (children) and is rendered under the general or special supervision of a licensed physician or surgeon selected by the above named persons or physician of their choice.

This authorization shall remain in effect until _____ (Date) unless revoked in writing and delivered by me.

_____ (Parent or Legal Guardian) _____ (Date)

_____ (Witness) _____ (Date)
Child's date of birth_____
Current medications _____

_____

Previous surgeries _____

_____

Current medical problems _____

_____

Last tetanus booster _____
Allergies to medications _____
Medications known to cause side effects for your child _____

263

APPENDIX B

MEDICAL INFORMATION FORM

This form should be taken to every physician office visit.

Name _____ Age _____ Date _____

Name of health insurance plan _____

Health insurance company's phone number _____

List of past surgeries _____, _____, _____
_____, _____, _____

Past hospitalizations _____, _____, _____
_____, _____

List of chronic medical problems (i.e. diabetes, hypertension) _____

_____, _____, _____

Names of specialists I am currently seeing for medical care and the medical problem he/she is treating.

    1. Dr. & Specialty_____ medical problem_____

    2. Dr. & Specialty_____ medical problem_____

    3. Dr. & Specialty_____ medical problem_____

    4. Dr. & Specialty_____ medical problem_____

Current medications:

Drug's name   Reason For Drug Use (or diagnosis)   Dosage (frequency & strength)

    1. _____

    2. _____

265

3. _____

4. _____

5. _____

6. _____

Pharmacy name and phone number _____

Drugs causing **ALLERGIC** reactions _____

Drugs causing side effects _____

Persons to Notify: _____

phone_____(work)_____(home)_____(cell phone)

APPENDIX C

CURRENT PREVENTIVE HEALTH CARE AND SAFETY RECOMMENDATIONS THAT SHOULD BE CONDUCTED BY YOUR PHYSICIAN OR HIS STAFF

Prenatal Guidelines (during pregnancy):

1) Complete health history at time of first obstetrical visit to include family, social, genetic, obstetric and dietary history.
2) Discussion of tobacco, alcohol, drug usage, and prior history of genital herpes.
3) A complete physical exam and PAP smear on first visit.
4) Weight obtained and recorded, urine test for glucose and albumin at each prenatal visit.
5) Repeat physical exam every 4 weeks until the 28th week of pregnancy.
6) At each 4 week visit, evaluate blood pressure, weight, size of uterus and fetal heart rate
7) Between weeks 28 and 36, see obstetrician every 2-3 weeks
8) After 36 weeks, see physician weekly: more often, if problems are occurring.
9) Multiple vitamins with folic acid should be taken daily once pregnancy begins.
10) Review of nutrition and good eating habits with physician.
11) Child birth and parenting classes.
12) Discussions about exercise, activity level and sexual activity.
13) Issues and questions about breast feeding.
14) Discussions concerning the WARNING signs and symptoms of labor.
15) Use of seat belts and avoidance of second hand smoke.

16) Avoidance of high risk activities such as water skiing, horseback riding, motorcycle riding, and skydiving.

17) Immunizations: If your blood type indicates that you are *rh negative*, you may need Rho (D) immunoglobulin at 28 weeks of gestation (pregnancy) to prevent blood incompatibility problems between you and your fetus.

Lab Studies usually performed with onset of pregnancy:

1) Hematocrit and hemoglobin studies to check for anemia at first visit and at week 30 of your pregnancy.

2) At first visit, a urinalysis and blood tests to include blood typing, Rh antibody screen (if Rh negative), tests for syphilis, hepatitis B, rubella, urinalysis with microscopic exam and routine cervical cultures for gonorrhea and chlamydia.

3) HIV screen is recommended.

4) Uterine ultrasound as needed.

5) Fetal heart tones recorded after 10 weeks of pregnancy.

6) Uterine size recorded after 20 weeks of pregnancy.

7) Glucose challenge test between weeks 24-28 to check for diabetes of pregnancy.

8) Test and if necessary treat for Group B strep between weeks 35-37 of pregnancy.

9) Repeat gonorrhea screening near end of pregnancy for women at risk.

10) African-Americans should have hemoglobin electrophoresis to check for sickle cell disease.

11) Triple check blood test for Alpha-fetoprotein, Unconjugated Estriol, and Human Chorionic Gonadotropin are tests that should be done between the 15th and 20th weeks of pregnancy to check for nervous system defects and genetic disorders such as Down's syndrome

12) In patients ages 35 and over other tests for Down's syndrome may be indicated.

Ages Birth - Until 2 Years

1) Newborn exam with medical and family history.
2) Antibiotic eye drops at birth.
3) Six physical exams in the first year and two exams in the second year.
4) Measure height, weight, head circumference with each visit and compare to normal standards.
5) Tuberculosis skin test can be repeated annually for high-risk children.
6) Hearing evaluation prior to age 18 months.
7) Hemoglobin once during infancy to check for anemia.
8) Lead level once during infancy and at age 2 years. Screen high risk children at first visit.
9) Thyroid blood tests between 3-6 days after birth.
10) Phenylalanine test 3-6 days after birth to check for genetic problem.
11) Hemoglobin electrophoresis blood test for sickle cell diseases if indicated.
12) Daily vitamins (sometimes with iron and or fluoride supplements).
13) Counseling parents on breast feeding, iron rich diet, accident prevention, and avoidance of smoking around children.
14) Sickle cell screening for high risk infants.
15) Periodic history regarding child's ability to hear.
16) Eye screening for newborn to 3 months and 6 months to one year of age.

Immunizations:

Hepatitis B - first dose given at birth, second dose 1-4 months later, third dose 6-18 months after second dose

If mother is positive for Hepatitis B, then Hepatitis B Immune globulin and Hepatitis B vaccine should be given at a separate site on the newborn. When a mother is positive for Hepatitis B then the first dose of the vaccine is

given at birth to the newborn, second dose given
at 1-2 months and 3rd dose at 6 months

DTaP or similar vaccine - given at ages 2 months, 4
months, 6 months and between 15-18 months

IPV (inactivated poliovirus vaccine) - given at 2 months,
4 months, and between 6-18 months

OPV (oral polio vaccine) **is no longer recommended**,
because it can in rare cases cause polio in
household contacts.

MMR (measles, mumps, rubella) - given once at age 12-
15 months

Hib-hemophilus influenza type b (to reduce risks of
meningitis) - given at 2 months, 4 months, 6
months and once between 12-15 months

Varicella zoster (chicken pox) vaccine once between 1-
18 months

Child Safety Issues:
1) **Child safety car seats***
2) Smoke detectors
3) Hot water heater temperature less than 120 degrees F
to avoid burns from scalding water
4) Stairway gates, electrical outlet guards, pool fence
5) Storage of drugs and toxic chemicals
6) Syrup of Ipecac on hand with poison control
telephone number written on bottle
7) Avoid passive smoking

* A recent study by The National Safe Kids Campaign found
that 86% of child safety seats were incorrectly used in the
state of Ohio, according to an article in *The Plain Dealer*,
February 13, 2000. The three most common forms of
misuse noted upon inspection of children sitting in their
seats included:

1) safety belts were not holding seats securely

270

2) harness straps were not snugly placed about the child's body
3) harness straps were not correctly routed

There are new inspection sights placed around the country where child safety seats can be inspected for damage and recalls. Parents will be shown how to use and install seats correctly. They will be shown how to select the correct safety seat based on a child's age, height and weight. In the US, there are over 4,600 certified child passenger safety technicians available for help and information. Please look in the appendix under Internet web sights for the National Highway Traffic Safety Administration web sight on how to locate the nearest safety technician or inspection station.

Ages 2-6 Years:
1) Medical history and physical exam once a year.
2) Measure height and weight annually.
3) Measure blood pressure starting at age 3.
4) Examine for cross eyes or failure to track simultaneously with both eyes starting ate age 2.
5) Visual acuity at age 3 and at age 5 years.
6) Hearing test starting at age 4 and then as needed based on hearing history
7) Tuberculosis skin test once between ages 4-6 years.
8) Lead level testing if indicated at age 12 months and 24 months.
9) Urinalysis at age 5 years.
10) Dental exam beginning at age 3 years.
11) Fluoride supplements if not available in water supply.
12) Sickle cell screening once during infancy or childhood, based on family history or genetics.

Immunizations:
1) DTaP or similar vaccine once between ages 4-6 years of age

2) IPV(inactivated polio virus vaccine) once between ages 4-6 years
3) Second MMR between ages 4-6 years
4) Varicella zoster(chickenpox)vaccine given once between 12 months and 12 years
5) Influenza (FLU) vaccine for high-risk patients (chronically ill)
6) Pneumococcal vaccine for high-risk patients (those that are chronically ill)
7) Hepatitis B vaccine given to those not previously immunized

Education:
1) Look for sources of lead in paints and plaster
2) Proper nutrition
3) Injury prevention at home and in vehicles
4) Effects of exposure from passive cigarette smoke
5) Avoidance of excess sun exposure and the use of sun screens
6) Child safety seats and seat belts
7) Keep hot water-heater temperature less than 120 degrees F
8) Electrical cords and outlets
9) Warning about strangers
10) Safety helmets
11) Pool fence
12) Proper storage of gasoline, matches, firearms, and chemicals
13) Syrup of ipecac with poison control phone number
14) Proper dental hygiene

Ages 7-12 Years:
1) Medical history and physical exam every other year until age 12
2) Height, weight, and blood pressure with each exam
3) Vision and hearing tests as needed
4) Evaluate stages of sexual development

5) Urinalysis once between 5-12 years of age
6) Cholesterol level once
7) Second MMR if not given earlier
8) Varicella vaccine once, if not given earlier
9) Hepatitis B series if not given earlier
10) Td (tetanus and diphtheria toxoids) given at age 11-12 years, if 5 years have passed since last childhood diphtheria, tetanus and pertussis vaccines were given
11) Influenza (FLU) vaccine and or Pneumococcal vaccine if needed (ask physician)
12) Tuberculosis skin test if at risk
13) Fluoride supplements if lacking in water supply

Education:
1) Proper diet and nutrition
2) Regular daily exercise
3) Avoidance of substance abuse: tobacco, alcohol, and illicit drugs
4) Discussion of sex education and menstrual issues
5) Proper dental hygiene
6) Use of sunscreens
7) **Use of car seat belts**, safety helmets, and proper protective gear for sports
8) Avoidance of firearms, matches, and toxic chemicals
9) Working smoke detectors

Ages 13-18 Years:
1) Medical history and physical exams annually
2) Height, weight, blood pressure annually
3) Staging of sexual development
4) Pelvic exam and PAP test after first episode of sexual intercourse or at age 18, whichever comes first
5) Testicular exam every year beginning at age 18 years. Teach self examination

Lab Testing:
1) Tuberculosis skin test if needed

2) Hemoglobin test for anemia in menstruating adolescents
3) Urinalysis if sexually active
4) Rubella antibody level in females of child bearing age if they lack evidence of immunity
5) Cholesterol level if indicated
6) Tests for STDs if indicated

Immunizations:

1) Tetanus diphtheria (Td) once between ages 11-16 years
2) Hepatitis B vaccine series if not previously received
3) If not immune give Varicella zoster (chicker pox) vaccine, 2 doses 4-8 weeks apart
4) Influenza vaccine and pneumococcal vaccine if needed

Education:
1) Monthly testicular exam by patient, or monthly self breast exam
2) Proper nutrition
3) Daily exercise
4) Avoidance of alcohol, tobacco products and illicit drugs
5) Avoidance of STDs, drunk driving
6) Use of safety belts, safety helmets, protective sports gear
7) Firearm safety
8) Use of sunscreen
9) Working smoke detectors
10) Education about unintended pregnancy

Ages 19-39 Years:
1) Medical history and physical exam every 3 years
2) Pelvic exam, PAP test and Breast exam annually

3) Height, weight, blood pressure with routine physical exams
4) Testicular and thyroid gland evaluation with physical exams
5) Blood pressure measured every 2 years
6) Glaucoma screening every 3 years in African-Americans ages 20-39 years

Immunizations:
1) Tetanus diphtheria every 8-10 years
2) Varicella Vaccine if not immune 2 doses 4-8 weeks apart
3) Influenza vaccine and pneumococcal vaccine if indicated
4) Hepatitis B series if not received earlier
5) Rubella vaccine for adults and nonpregnant women without evidence of immunity

Lab Tests Average Risk Patients:
Total cholesterol and HDL (good) cholesterol every 5 years

Lab Tests: High Risk Patients:
Urinalysis, fasting blood sugar, cholesterol level, hemoglobin level and tests for STDs
HIV screening as indicated by behavior

Patient Education:
1) Monthly testicular or breast self exams
2) Discussions about nutrition and exercise
3) Discussions about contraception and preventing STDs
4) Avoidance of alcohol, tobacco and substance abuse
5) Proper dental health
6) Proper use of seat belts, safety helmets and sports protective gear
7) Firearm safety

8) Working smoke detectors
9) Proper use of sun screens
10) Review proper medications and their dosages
11) Education about unintended pregnancy

Ages 40-64 Years:

1) Medical and family history every 2 years
2) Physical examination every 1-2 years
3) For patients age 50 and over, an examination of the sigmoid colon every 5 years with a flexible scope or an air contrast barium enema every 5-10 years or a colonoscopy every 10 years to examine the large bowel for evidence of colon cancer
4) Colonoscopy beginning at age 40 and over, with family history of colon cancer or polyps
5) Digital rectal exam annually age 40 and over
6) Prostate exam annually age 40 and over with history of vasectomy
7) Prostate exam annually age 50 and over for non-vasectomized males.
8) Mammogram every year for age 40 and over
9) Pelvic exam annually
10) Breast exam annually
11) Thyroid exam annually for age 40 and over
12) Vision testing every 2 years for age 40 and over (diabetics should be evaluated annually)
13) Hearing testing every 2 years for age 50 and over as indicated
14) Evaluation for carotid artery bruits (abnormal sounds that indicate possible blockage in your arteries, increasing the risk of stroke)
15) Glaucoma screening every 2 years

Laboratory tests:

1) Prostate specific antigen level (PSA) annually for age 50 and over. If patient has had vasectomy

276

before the age of 35, a PSA level should be done every 1 to 2 years for ages 40 and over (this is my recommendation and not one of any national organization and would be therefore controversial).

2) Stool tests for blood every year for patients ages 50 and over
3) Pap smear every 1 to 3 years
4) Total cholesterol, HDL (good) cholesterol, and LDL (bad) cholesterol every 2 to 3 years
5) Urinalysis every 2 years
6) Fasting blood sugar every 2 years to check for diabetes
7) If sexually active and not in a monogamous relationship, test for sexually transmitted diseases (STDs) including tests for syphilis, chlamydia, gonorrhea, AIDS, hepatitis B and C, herpes and human papilloma virus after discussing your options with your physician
8) Bone mineral content to evaluate for osteoporosis as determined by physician.
9) Evaluation of moles and suspicious skin lesions

Patient Education:
1) Dental care and flossing
2) Exercise
3) Alcohol, tobacco and illegal drug use
4) Nutrition
5) Sunlight exposure
6) Contraception and STDs
7) Seat belt use
8) Helmet safety
9) Hot water temperature below 120 degrees F
10) Use of smoke detectors
11) Use of medication to prevent osteoporosis
12) Use of aspirin to lower risk of strokes and heart attacks
13) Vitamin E 400 IU's per day to decrease prostate cancer and other diseases

14) Review of medication and proper dosages
15) Avoidance of passive tobacco smoke

Immunizations:
1) Tetanus diphtheria every 10 years
2) Pneumococcal vaccine if indicated
3) Influenza vaccine if indicated
4) Varicella vaccine if not immune
5) Hepatitis B series if not immune
6) Rubella vaccine for adults and non pregnant women without evidence of immunity

Ages 65 and over:
1) Annual medical history, physical exam, and blood pressure reading
2) Examination of the sigmoid colon every 5 years, or an air contrast barium enema every 5-10 years or a colonoscopy every 10 years to examine the large bowel for evidence of colon cancer.
3) Colonoscopy if there is a family history of colon polyps or colon cancer
4) Rectal exam, prostate exam, and breast exam annually
5) Pelvic exam once a year
6) Tests for blood in stool annually
7) Glaucoma testing annually
8) Annual mammogram
9) Self-testicular exam or breast exam monthly
10) Annual thyroid exam for thyroid nodules
11) Annual carotid artery evaluation to help prevent strokes
12) Tuberculosis skin tests if indicated
13) Bone density determination every 2 to 3 years for women and as indicated for men

Lab Tests:
1) P.S.A. level (prostatic specific antigen) annually

2) Total cholesterol, LDL (bad) cholesterol, HDL (good) cholesterol, urinalysis, and fasting blood sugar tests annually
3) Thyroid tests for women annually

Immunizations:
1) Tetanus-diphtheria booster every 8-10 years
2) Varicella Vaccine if not immune, 2 doses given 4-8 weeks apart
3) Pneumococcal Vaccine once every 8-10 years
4) Influenza Vaccine annually
5) Hepatitis B series if not immune

Education:
1) Proper nutrition and exercise levels
2) Safety in the home
3) Avoidance of substance abuse
4) Proper dental hygiene
5) Use of sunscreens
6) Prevention of falls and use of canes when needed
7) Use of safety belts
8) Hot water heater setting below 120 degrees F
9) Use of hormone replacement therapy or treatment of osteoporosis when needed

What's On The Horizon? According to the American Medical News, January 17, 2000, this year 68,000 women will die from lung cancer, double the rate of breast cancer deaths. Studies are on going that indicate that CT (computed tomography) scans may be able to detect even small lung cancers not visible on chest x-ray.

The Early Lung Cancer Action Program studied 1000 smokers (459 women and 541 men) with a median age of 67 years and a median smoking history of 45 years. Thirty-one tumors were detected by CT scans. Only 7 of these were found by x-ray studies. In long term moderate to heavy smokers, CT scans may be more valuable than a chest x-ray to screen for early lung cancer.

This technology will not be widely used unless the cost of the procedure can be covered. Possibly money obtained from the tobacco companies through state litigation can be used to offset these costs.

Appendix D

Preventive Health Questionnaire and Worksheet

Name_____ **Date**_____

Information that should be monitored on a regular basis by adult patients:

Last complete physical examination.   date_____

Last PAP test and female evaluation.   date_____

Last breast exam   date_____

Last prostate examination.   date_____

Last mammogram.   date_____

Last test for blood in stool   date_____

Last sigmoidoscopy.   date_____

Last chest x-ray.   date_____

Last electrocardiogram.   date_____

Last cholesterol blood test.   date_____

Last routine eye examination.   date_____

Last dental examination and teeth   date_____
    cleaning.

Last tetanus booster.   date_____

Last influenza shot (flu shot).   date_____

APPENDIX E

SOCIAL AND ENVIRONMENTAL ISSUES THAT
IMPACT ON HEALTH STATUS

The following are subjects that will influence your health and should be clarified at some point with your primary care physician.

Check those that apply:

Married___ Single___ Separated___ Divorced___ Widowed___ Gay___

Check current marital status if it applies:
First marriage___ Second marriage___ Third marriage___

Do you live in an:
Apartment___ Home___ Condominium___ Other dwelling___
Age of Dwelling_____

Pets:
Dog___ Cat___ bird___ reptile___ other_____

Sleeping arrangement:
Sleeps with significant other: ___ yes ___no If no, Why not?____
_____

Sleeping furniture:
mattress and springs___ age of bedding in years____ waterbed___

Foreign travel:
Countries visited in the past two years:_____
Countries visited in your lifetime:_____

Military status:
never served in military_____
veteran_____ branch of service_____ stationed in US_____
stationed in foreign land_____

Vehicle safety:
wears seat belts___ does not wear seat belts___
vehicle has air bags____ vehicle does not have air bags___

283

vehicle has anti-lock brakes___ vehicle does not have anti-lock brakes___

has been instructed in the use of anti-lock brakes?___yes _____no

vehicle has **safe**: tires___ wipers___ effective brakes___ working lights___

Alcohol and recreational drug use:

beer____ wine____ mixed drinks____ marijuana____ other_____

frequency of use_____ quantity of use per day or week_____

Tobacco use:

cigarettes____ cigars____ pipe____ smokeless tobacco____

quantity of the above used per day_____

Coffee use:___ regular___ decaf___ cups per day_____

tea use:_____ cups per day_____

Women: does monthly self breast exam ____yes ____no

Men: does monthly testicular exam ____yes _____no

Diet: avoids excessive fats in diet ___yes ___no

Avoids salt in diet ___yes ___no

Floss teeth daily ____yes _____no

APPENDIX F

HEALTH AND MEDICAL RELATED
INTERNET WEB SIGHTS

acne. **For teens:** Weekly acne news, tips, advice, personal stories and the opportunity to e-mail a doctor for personalized information
www. facefacts.com/ac/index.htm

allergies and asthma. ga-zoon --tite
A company that specializes in products reviewed by the Medical Advisory Board for patients who suffer from allergies and or asthma
www.gazoontite.com

American Academy of Family Practice.
Patient information web sight available
www.aafp.org

American Medical Association.
AMA web sight
www.ama-assn.org

antibiotic use.
The prudent use of antibiotics
The alliance for prudent use of antibiotics
www.apua.org/

Alliance for the Prudent Use of Antibiotics.
www.antibiotic.org

aromatherapy. Information about aromatherapy
www.healthy.net/clinic/therapy/aroma/

arthritis. Arthritis treatments, research, and support group information
www.arthritis.org/
www.pslgroup.com/arthritis.htm

asthma. An excellent magazine designed to provide information for readers interested in the problem of asthma
Asthma Magazine
www. letters@asthmamagazine.com

asthma management.
How to diagnose, manage and avoid asthma triggers
http://healthtalk.com/aen/110999/replay.html

attention deficit disorder and hyperactivity.
Attention Deficit and Hyperactivity Disorder:
History, diagnosis, causes, and treatments including side effects of medications
http://healthology.com/focus webcast.asp?f=children&c=childadhd1

cancer (30 varieties).
30 varieties of cancer reviewed, message boards, a bookstore, and daily news
www. cancereducation.com

cancer pain relief. Cancer Pain Information Center
www.cancer pain relief.com/cancer pain

cancer (prostate). Prostate cancer tailored to meet each patient's needs. News, general information, support groups
www. cancer facts. com/portal.asp? From Login=True & Cancer TypeId=1

.

Prostate cancer, related products and support resources hosted by Astra Zeneca
www.prostrateinfo.com

Center for Disease Control and Prevention.
Emerging Infectious diseases home page
www.cdc.gov/ncidod/EID/eid,htms

childbirth.
Pain control during childbirth: What are your options?
Many issues and questions answered by a panel of experts
http://healthology.com/focuswebcast.asp?f=pregnancy&c =preg pain1

child- rearing.
Parent to parent, a sight devoted to child-rearing questions
www.p2ptips@att.net

child safety seats.
How to locate the nearest safety technician or child safety seat inspection sight
The National Highway Traffic Safety Administration
www.nhtsa.dot.gov

Cholesterol elevation.
Sponsored by Park-Davis, helpful information, cholesterol worksheet and healthy diet guidelines
www.parke-davis.com/version4/cholest.html

communication with your doctor.
How to talk to your doctor. A websight sponsored by the American Association of Retired People (AARP)
www.aarp.org/confacts/health/talkdr.html

287

disabled patients (this sight is accessible to the blind).
A web sight devoted to the disabled so that they may live fuller and more satisfying lives
www.wemedia.com

erectile dysfunction.
Understanding erectile dysfunction, The American Medical Association's websight for the causes, diagnosis, and treatment of erectile dysfunction
www.ama-assn.org/insight/spec con/sexdysf/index.htm

exercise.
Here's the SKINNY. "Shape Up And Drop 10", "Shape Up America"
www.shapeup.org

headaches.
Migraine headaches and tension headaches
www.4 woman.gov/faq/migraine.htm

Headaches: Self-care Flow Chart
The American Academy of Family Physicians sponsors a headache question flow chart, possible diagnoses, and recommended courses of action
www.aafp.org/medguide/charts/topic2.html

health channels.
CBS Healthwatch
Delivers good information that can be customized to a patient's needs; Twenty-two health channels, a library and health professionals are available to answer questions
http://healthwatch.medscape.com

health issues.
Comprehensive health issues for everyone covering many health issues, diseases,

288

treatments, procedures, vaccinations and travel health. On-call pediatrician available to respond to questions
www.adam.com

heart disease. The American Heart Association
www.american heart.org

health related topics.
Health related internet resources
www.social.com/health/

health sciences. Internet resources related to the health sciences
www.hdcn.com

immunizations. The Center for Disease Control(CDC) Information about available vaccines
www.cdc.gov/nip/publications/VIS/default.htm.

kidney disease. American Association of Kidney Patients
www.aakp.org

multiple sclerosis. Multiple Sclerosis Education Network
www.healthtalk.com/msen/msp/111199program.html

nervous system disorders.
National Institute of Neurological Disorders and Stroke
www.ninds.nih.gov.

nutrition. Information about vitamins, minerals, carbohydrates, proteins, fats, and fiber
http://web.bu.edu/COHIS/nutrtion/nutri.htm

peptic ulcer disease,

> Information about peptic ulcer disease, heartburn, esophagitis and other problems associated with excess stomach acid secretion.
> Sponsored by TAP Pharmaceuticals
> **www.prevacid.com**

prevention.

> Information about communicable diseases, health risks, injuries and disabilities, prevention and travel tips
> **www.cdc.gov/**

public health.

> Information related to public health; The National Institutes of Health
> **www.nih.gov/**

relaxation techniques.

> Relaxation techniques to soothe the psyche and relieve stress
> **www.shsw.edu/~counsel/shortr.html**

sleep and snoring disorders.

> Sleep disorders including snoring, sleep deprivation, insomnia, and restless leg syndrome
> **www.newtechpub.com/**
> **www.sleepnet.com/**

walking and exercise.

> Information about power walking, race walking, exercise and leisure
> **www.teleport.com/~walking/walking.shtml**

women's health. Women's health, from migraines to menopause
> **www.womens-health.com**

A sight devoted to motherhood and to share the "essential bond of motherhood"
www.myria.com

The Doctor Will See You Now
Specialists review common conditions, bioethics, women's health, and senior health
www.the doctor will see you now.com

World Health. World Health Organization
Operates under the auspices of the United Nation
www.who.ch/

yoga. Information and group discussions about yoga
www.ijoga.com/yf/

APPENDIX G

Paying the Piper: Preventing and Correcting
Medical Insurance Problems

After receiving medical care, whether it be at a physician's office, a laboratory, x-ray facility or a hospital, bills will have to be paid either by you or your insurance company. Preventing problems early on will reduce your chances of incurring unexpected costs that should be paid for by health insurance.

Following a few simple principles will go a long way in this arena.

1. When applying for new insurance, declare all pre-existing conditions. If you have not disclosed pre-existing conditions prior to beginning a new insurance plan, your insurance company can deny payment for those conditions when the time comes.

2. Become intimately aware of details within your health insurance policy.

3. Establish a relationship with a PCP that is part of your health plan before a crisis occurs.

4. If your physician is in a group practice, be sure that his partners are also included under your health insurance policy. Should you have to see a partner when your PCP is not available, inquire about the possibility of billing under your doctor's name for services provided.

5. Do not go to an emergency room without permission from your PCP except in a life or limb threatening situation.

6. Do not pay a medical bill until receiving an explanation of benefits form from your insurance company. In the interest

293

of efficiency, doctor's offices often send out patient bills on a weekly basis before an insurance company has received a claim.

In about 15-20% of cases, doctor's offices submit incorrect billing codes resulting in denial of benefits. The bill can be resubmitted using correct billing codes and data.

Should an error be detected after reviewing the explanation of benefits form received from your insurance company, call the office and ask to speak with a billing specialist.

7. Ask for an itemized bill for all costs associated with a hospital stay.

8. Do not pay for services not provided nor supplies and medications not utilized.

Insurance companies sometimes pay discounted rates to hospitals based on pre-arranged contracts. Be sure that the co-pays you are responsible for are adjusted to discounted rates.

9. At some hospitals, radiologists and pathologists bill independently of the hospital and forward a bill to you. Be sure that these individuals have access to your insurance information so they can initially bill your primary or secondary insurance companies.

10. When contesting a bill, keep a log of conversations between you and office, hospital or insurance account representatives.

Send important correspondence by certified mail and request a return receipt.

11. For those of you that feel uncomfortable with handling insurance disputes, hire a patient billing advocate to go to bat for you.

Large medical institutions such as The Cleveland Clinic Foundation have their own patient advocates, ombudsmen, and billing specialists that can assist you with payment disputes or other problems associated with the delivery of your health care.

12. The Alliance of Claims Assistance Professionals in Chicago will find a member of their organization in your area should you be faced with a questionable medical bill of significant magnitude. These professionals charge an hourly or flat fee for their services.

Contact the Alliance of Claims Assistance Professionals at 877-275-876

APPENDIX H

A Prayer for Life and Eternal Health

Dear Father:

You have given me a magnificent body.
A machine finer than any man could ever build.
I shall not squander its form or beauty through carelessness nor laziness.
I shall protect it from danger through safe practices such as seatbelt use and safe sex.
I will protect it from the harmful effects of illicit drugs, tobacco, and alcohol abuse.
Good nutrition, proper exercise and adequate sleep, will give me strength and grace.
Sensible use of medications, herbs, and vitamins will replenish lost elements and strengthen weakened organs.
Most importantly, preventive health shall be practiced and sound medical wisdom followed.
Believing that good health is not a right, but an achievement won each day I live,
I will follow these ideals throughout my journey, until with You I reach perfection; and then unite with all the souls who have gone before me.

Philip Caravella

APPENDIX I

Phone Numbers of National Health Organizations

Alzheimers's Association 1-800-272-3900

American Association of Retired Person's (AARP)......1-800-424-3410

American Cancer Society 1-800-227-2345

American Diabetes Association 1-800-232-3472

American Heart Association 1-800-242-8721

American Kidney Foundation 1-800-622-9010

American Liver Foundation 1-800-233-0179

American Lung Association 1-800-586-4872

American Parkinson's Disease Association 1-800-223-2732

Arthritis Foundation Information Hotline 1-800-283-7800

Better Hearing Institute; Hearing Helpline ....1-800-EAR WELL

Medicare Telephone Hotline 1-800-638-6833

National Council on Alcoholism & Drug Dependence .1-800-622-2255

National Institute on Aging Information Center 1-800-222-2225

National Mental Health Association 1-800-969-6642

National Osteoporosis Foundation 1-800-223-9994

National Stroke Association 1-800-STROKES

The Lighthouse --for the visually impaired 1-800-334-5497

GLOSSARY

acuity. in focus, sharpness of one vision.

advocate. someone who speaks in favor or something or someone and supports a specific position.

air cast. a rigid splint with a built in air cushion used to assist in the treatment of a sprained ankle.

Alpha-fetoprotein. a fetal blood protein found normally in amniotic fluid with high levels indicating nervous system defects (neural tube defects) and very low levels associated with Down's Syndrome.

amoxicillin. a commonly used antibiotic.

ampicillin. a commonly used antibiotic.

antibiotic. a medicine used to fight bacterial infections.

antibody. a protein developed by the body's immune system to defeat a foreign substance invasion.

antivenom. an antitoxin used to destroy or neutralize a venom or poison.

apaneurosis. a thick fibrous membrane which wraps around the base of the skull and then projects upward towards the top of the skull.

bacteria. a microscopic organism

beta blockers. a category of drugs with multiple uses; most frequently used to treat high blood pressure

bioavailability. the availability of a substance used in a biologic activity at a specific site in the body

bioequivalent. how one drug product may compare to another in strength or activity.

cancer. a tumor that expands and spreads killing its host if left unchecked.

carpal tunnel syndrome. a defect with the median nerve at the level of the wrist often causing numbness of the fingers or hands frequently occurring at night or during repetitive hand activities.

CT scan. a cross sectional computerized x-ray image of a body part, organ, or section.

chlamydia. a parasitic organism associated with several diseases by infecting the eye, genital tract or rectum.

Chlamydia psittaci. a specific dangerous form of chlamydia associated with disease.

cholesterol. a group of fatty substances that when abnormally elevated causes blood vessel and heart disease.

colonoscope. a flexible 120 cm. long instrument passed into the rectum used to view the inside of the colon or large bowel in search of abnormalities such as colon cancer.

colonoscopy. the procedure performed with a colonoscope to search for diseases of the colon.

copay. a fee required by a health insurance company that a patient must pay as their share of a service performed or a prescription filled.

cortisol. a substance formed in the adrenal glands useful in several processes that occur within the body.

Cushing's Syndrome. a disorder related to the excess production of cortisol. If left untreated it may lead to death from high blood pressure, heart disease, infection and even suicide.

Deductible. the amount of money annually required of a medical insurance policy holder before full financial benefits can be achieved.

Diabetes. a metabolic disorder associated with excess blood sugar levels due to a lack of insulin or ineffectiveness of existing insulin.

differential diagnosis. a list of possible problems that could be the cause of a group of symptoms a patient has.

diagnostic techniques. for our purposes, methods used to evaluate for specific disorders or medical problem.

Down's Syndrome. mongolism caused by a chromosomal abnormality resulting in characteristic facial changes, short fingers, widened spaces between the first and second digits of the hands and feet, accompanied by mental retardation.

enterococcus. a family of bacteria that live in the intestine.

epiglottitis. a lid shaped organ that covers the opening to the larynx or voice box.

erythematosus. a redness of the skin.

fluoride. a compound with fluorine.

formulary. a list of standard medications given preferred status for use by enrollees of a health insurance plan.

gastroenterologist. a physician that specializes in medical problems associated with the digestive tract.

geriatric medicine. a speciality that deals with the elderly.

general practitioner. a physician who provides medical care in a limited fashion based on his level of education and experience. He is not considered a specialist nor has he completed formal post graduate medical education beyond an internship.

generic drugs. a basic drug no longer patent protected that can be marketed under any name selected by a pharmaceutical company for commercial distribution if it meets FDA approval.

gestation. the period of time during which a fetus develops within the uterus.

glomerulonephritis. an inflammatory process caused by the bacteria responsible for strep throat that adversely affects subunits of the kidney which may eventually lead to kidney failure.

Group A beta-hemolytic streptococcus. the bacteria responsible for strep throat and related diseases such as scarlet fever, rheumatic fever, and glomerulonephritis.

health maintenance organization (HMO). an insurance plan that provides a full range of medical and preventive health services through a primary care physician associated by contract with specific hospitals and pharmacies.

hematocrit. the volume of red blood cells found in whole blood cells.

hemoglobin. a pigment in the red blood cell that carries oxygen. There are different forms of hemoglobin as in fetal hemoglobin, the predominant form found in the newborn.
> Hemoglobin A is the predominant form found in adult red blood cells. Measuring hemoglobin levels is a common method to check for anemia or blood loss.

high blood pressure. a blood pressure considered above normal based on a patient's age.

Hippocratic Oath. an ancient oath taken by physicians upon graduation to hold certain ethical standards and principles.

Human Chorionic Gonadotropin. a substance that is present during pregnancy and can also be a marker for certain forms of tumors.

ibuprofen. a common medication taken to reduce pain, inflammation, and fever.

ICU. intensive care unit.

immunization. an inoculation used to promote protection against a foreign substance capable of causing disease.

influenza. a common viral illness associated with fatigue, fever, muscle aches, loss of appetite, headache and cough.

intravenous. within a vein.

intubate. to place a breathing tube past the glottis into the larynx so that air or oxygen can pass into the lungs.

laryngeal tumor. a tumor of the larynx or voice box.

Lyme Disease. a disease caused by the organism Borrelia burgdorferi, passed by the bite of the Ixodid tick and associated "with a viral-like syndrome", rash, neck pain, red throat, joint pain, and preceded by an area of reddish concentric circles referred to as a "bull's eye" pattern.

mammogram. an x-ray of the breast used to diagnose breast cancer.

managed care plan. a health insurance plan that controls how medical care is dispensed to its enrollees.

mitral valve prolapse (MVP) syndrome. the most common form of congenital heart defect; usually patients are without symptoms. MVP is often associated with palpitations, anxiety, fatigue, lightheadedness and sometimes chest pain.

modalities. therapeutic agents used by physical therapists to treat painful muscles, joints or other muscle skeletal structures of the body.

MRI. magnetic resonant imaging- a computerized method of viewing many tissues within the body to search for tumors or other defects without the need of x-rays.

naproxen sodium. a common medication taken to reduce pain and inflammation of muscles and joints.

nurse practitioner. defined by Catherine Holzheimer, RN,-a registered nurse with both an advanced education (a master's degree or Ph.D.) and the clinical competency necessary for the delivery of primary health and medical care. They are licensed by the state in which they practice.

obstetrics. the medical specialty associated with the management of pregnant patients.

ophthalmologist. a physician and surgeon who treats diseases and surgical problems of the eyes.

optometrist. a Ph.D.. who can diagnose and treat less severe diseases and problems of the eyes.

optician. someone educated in the fitting, selling, and repairing of spectacles (eye glasses).

osteoporosis. a thinning and weakening of the bones which can lead to serious fractures.

otitis. an infection within the inner or outer ear.

otoscope. an instrument used to view the ear canal and the ear drum.

palpitations. irregular heart beats noticeable to a patient.

PAP test. Papanicolaou test, named after the man who described its use. Cells are scraped off the cervix of the uterus and placed on a glass slide where they can be evaluated for evidence of cancer and other abnormalities.

perineal. the perineum or the area involving the pelvic area of the female; in the male the area between scrotum and the anus.

phenylalanine. an amino acid required for growth in infants but is also utilized in adults as well.

physician's assistant. an individual that works along side a physician and under the collaborating physician's medical license.

postpartum. occurring after child birth.

PPO. preferred provider organization, a group of physicians that has contracted with a medical insurance company to provide health care to its enrollees.

precertification. the methodology used by health insurance companies to pre-approve a test, hospital visit or specialty referral.

Premenstrual Syndrome (PMS). a group of physical and emotional symptoms usually accompanied by behavioral changes preceding a menstrual period and later disappearing sometime after the period has begun.

primary care physician. a physician who is responsible for the general care of a patient, often coordinating other specialists and medical related activities required for over all management.

prostate gland. a male gland surrounding the neck of the bladder which manufactures a component of seminal fluid.

prostatic specific antigen (PSA). a natural occurring substance from the prostate gland that may become elevated in various diseases of the gland.

Pseudomonas aeruginosa. an infectious bacteria responsible for many potentially dangerous illnesses.

Rheumatic Fever. a cluster of signs and symptoms caused by Group A beta-hemolytic streptococci (the bacterial cause of strep throat) that may cause heart damage and nervous system changes.

Rh antibody. one of a group of protein substances occurring in the blood.

rhinitis. inflammation of the lining of the nose often associated with drainage from the nose or mucose deposited into the back of the throat.

Rh-negative. the absence in 15% of Caucasians of the D antigen, a protein like substance occurring in blood.

Rho (D) immunoglobutin. a specialized protein referred to as an antibody.

rotovirus. a infectious virus that that can inhabit the colon resulting in diarrhea.

Scarlet Fever. an infectious bacterial disease caused by strep throat and associated with a characteristic scarlet rash.

sigmoidoscope. a flexible 60-65 cm. long instrument used by physicians to view the inside of the lower or sigmoid colon.

sigmoidoscopy. a procedure using a sigmoidoscope to view the sigmoid colon.

staphylococcus aureus (staph). a bacteria notorious for causing many dangerous skin and wound infections.

strep throat. a throat infection caused by strains of the bacteria streptococcus.

Syrup of Ipecac. a medication used to induce vomiting in some cases of poisoning when recommended by a physician or a poison control center.

Temporal Mandibular Joint (TMJ) Syndrome. an inflammatory painful condition of the TMJ joint where the jaw is connected to the skull just anterior to the ear.

tetanus. a dangerous often lethal disease caused by an organism clostridium tetani, associated with severe muscle spasm and nervous system involvement.

tetanus diphtheria vaccine. a combination vaccine used to protect against tetanus and diphtheria infections.

thyroid gland. an endocrine gland located in the neck anterior to the trachea which manufactures thyroid hormones required for normal growth, maturation and function.

tuberculosis. a contagious and potentially lethal lung infection caused by the bacteria Mycobacterium tuberculosis.

ultrasound. a technology in which sound waves beyond the range of human hearing are passed through tissues (organs) of different densities to form an image used in looking for abnormal changes.

unconjugated estriol. a form of estrogen.

urinalysis. a study of the urine.

vaccination. immunizing someone with a weakened or incomplete substance so that the immune system will develop antibodies to protect the individual from an infectious disease.

varicella vaccine. a vaccine used to protect against diseases caused by varicella-zoster such as chicken pox and shingles.

virus. one of a group of infectious agents composed of either RNA or DNA proteins and are responsible for many diseases ranging from the common cold to AIDs.

INDEX

A

abdomen, 54, 82, 86, 108, 200, 203
abuse, 22, 37, 58, 102, 273, 275, 279, 297
acne, 86, 285
adolescents, 82, 104, 112, 128, 274
AIDs, 311
alcohol, 102, 267, 273, 274, 275, 297
allergies, 35, 104, 116, 117, 165, 166, 285
antibiotic, 54, 146, 183, 184, 185, 187, 218, 285, 301
antibodies, 165, 223, 310
antivenom, 301
appendicitis, 3
appointments, 67, 68, 70, 72, 79, 155, 241
art, xix, 7, 9, 11, 13, 15, 16, 45, 72, 105, 131, 157, 249
artist, viii, 38
aspirin, 165, 194, 202, 277
asthma, 75, 126, 285, 286

B

beta blockers, 301
bioavailability, 173, 302
bleeding, 165, 194, 202, 221
breast, 38, 73, 77, 105, 140, 143, 239, 267, 269, 274, 275, 278, 279, 281, 284, 306

C

carpal tunnel syndrome, 96, 302
cervix, 77, 138, 307
chaperone, 112
check-up, 73, 78
childbirth, 287
children, vii, xi, 5, 37, 38, 70, 82, 86, 93, 94, 104, 105, 107, 108, 109, 110, 111, 113, 126, 127, 180, 215, 217, 222, 225, 227, 251, 263, 269, 270, 286
chlamydia, 123, 139, 268, 277, 302
cholesterol, 12, 73, 136, 137, 158, 161, 163, 206, 207, 275, 277, 278, 281, 287, 302
circadian, 120
clothing, 82, 83, 112, 120, 209

313

formulary, 21, 174, 195, 304

G

generic, 4, 5, 21, 95, 173, 174, 175, 177, 304
genital, 105, 109, 110, 267, 302
gonorrhea, 139, 268, 277
guardian, 104, 112

H

headaches, 34, 35, 36, 84, 95, 166, 288
hepatitis, 141, 268, 277
Hippocrates, 184, 238, 6
hives, 54, 116, 165, 187
HMO, 23, 25, 27, 71, 153, 241, 245, 304, 6

I

ICU, 53, 54, 305
incompetent, 10, 100, 101, 251
infant, 223
injections, 49, 70, 105, 107, 223, 225
insurance, health, 19
international, 7, 169
internists, 38, 133
intimacy, 15
ipecac, 272

J

Johns Hopkins University, 81

K

kidney, 85, 119, 147, 148, 163, 191, 218, 289, 304

L

lawsuits, 112
life-threatening, 53, 119, 123, 154, 190
lightheaded, 221, 226, 231
luck, 240, 248, 259

M

N

O

P

pharmacists, 41, 83, 193, 194
pharmacy, 96, 169, 170
PMS, 127, 308
pneumonia, 122, 123, 124, 126, 131, 157, 212
poisonings, 180
polyps, 202, 204, 239, 276, 278
precertification, 26, 308
pregnancy, 37, 103, 267, 268, 274, 276, 287, 305
premenstrual syndrome, 127
prenatal, 267
prescriptions, 19, 42, 95, 96, 147, 153, 169, 177, 183, 189, 191, 192, 193
Prevacid, 176
PSA, 136, 139, 276, 308
psychological, 45, 46

R

rashes, 165, 187
Red Cross, 141
referral, 25, 41, 42, 55, 58, 61, 233, 308
research, vii, 46, 81, 136, 138, 139, 145, 170, 194, 223, 237, 286, 7
rhinitis, 75, 309

S

satisfaction scale, 148
scans, 22, 35, 135, 233, 243, 244, 279
scheduling, 26, 27, 63, 67, 68, 69, 70, 72, 73, 74, 76, 78, 79, 80, 89, 91, 93,
    122, 153, 157, 179, 241
science, 11, 13, 22, 67, 91, 136, 143, 157, 239, 249, 253, 255, 257, 259
self-diagnosis, 15, 123, 124
self-referral, 72
sigmoidoscopy, 202, 204, 281, 309
snoring, 290
Somalia, 224
specialist, 3, 4, 24, 33, 34, 35, 36, 38, 42, 53, 54, 55, 56, 57, 72, 83, 115, 117,
    142, 199, 200, 233, 249, 257, 294, 304
spouse, 99, 100, 102
STDs, 274, 275, 277
strep, 124, 146, 217, 218, 304, 309
streptococcus, 217, 304, 309
stroke, 148, 276
surrogate, 101
syphilis, 268, 277

317

T

teaching, 249
technology, 7, 22, 103, 140, 175, 279, 310
telephone, 151, 180, 241, 270
temperature, 119, 121, 270, 272, 277
temporal mandibular joint, 35
tests, 3, 10, 20, 23, 24, 33, 34, 35, 38, 56, 74, 78, 85, 103, 123, 132, 133, 135,
    136, 137, 138, 139, 140, 141, 142, 143, 147, 153, 165, 183, 191, 199, 200,
    201, 202, 205, 206, 207, 211, 221, 233, 238, 244, 255, 256, 268, 269, 272,
    275, 276, 277, 278
tetanus, 225, 263, 273, 281, 310
thin prep, 138
throat, 35, 53, 75, 109, 123, 124, 146, 176, 206, 211, 215, 216, 217, 218, 304,
    306, 309
ticklish, 108
tobacco, 267, 273, 274, 275, 277, 279, 284, 297
toys, 111
travelers, 169
tuberculosis, 119, 184, 212, 310

U

ultrasound, 61, 62, 85, 103, 140, 143, 244, 268, 310
urine, 89, 103, 135, 163, 206, 211, 212, 267, 310

V

vaccines, 223, 224, 225, 226, 227, 273, 289
Valium, 86, 174
Vanessa, 22, 34, 35
Viagra, 170
victims, 223

W

waiting rooms, 5, 111
Walther Cancer Research Center, 145
women, 11, 37, 38, 77, 82, 112, 126, 127, 136, 140, 143, 163, 231, 239, 247,
    268, 275, 278, 279, 290, 291
world-class, v, xvii, 7, 11, 191

AFTERWORD

Every effort has been made to accurately portray the facts and issues that pertain to many aspects of health care as it is delivered in an office setting. The primary thrust of the book , The Art Of Being A Patient, relates to how as a patient you will be better able to manage your personal health through knowledge, preparation, and assertiveness. Through the use of the tactics outlined within the book, you will be able to effectively influence your physician and the health care system resulting in better medical care and greater personal satisfaction.

Differences of opinion are always possible if not likely, as are inadvertent errors. I welcome your suggestions, comments and corrections in hopes that future editions can prove to be even more useful.

I can be reached at www.caravelmd@AOL.com

Philip Caravella, M.D.,F.A.A.F.P.

REFERENCES

1. Gerrity MS, Cole SA. Improving the Recognition and Management of Depression. J Fam Prac 1999; Vol. 48, No. 12 (Dec).

2. Leo RJ. Competency and the Capacity to Make Treatment Decisions: A Primer for Primary Care Physicians. Prim Care Companion, J Clin Psy 1999; Vol. 1, No. 5 (Oct).

3. Greider L. Talking Back to Your Doctor Works. AARP Bul 2000; Vol. 41, No. 2 (Feb).

4. Sison A. More Doctors Write Rx's Patients Request. Med Tribune 1999; (Dec).

5. Rivo L. Practicing in the New Millennium: Do You Have What It Takes? Fam Prac Management 2000; (Jan).

6. Tobin MJ. The Family Physician of the 21st Century: Guiding the Female Patient's Health Care. Female Patient 2000; Vol. 25, (Jan).

7. Appelbaum PS. Threats to the Confidentiality of Medical Records--No Place to Hide. JAMA 2000; Vol 283, No. 6 (Feb 9).

8. Approved Drug Products with Therapeutic Equivalence Evaluations. US Department of Health and Human Services, Public Health Service, Food and Drug Admin. 18th Edition, "Orange Book", 1998; (Jan).

9. Ruffin IV MT, Gorenflo DW, Woodman B. Predictors of Screening for Breast, Cervical, colorectal, and Prostatic Cancer Among Community-Based Primary Care Practices. J Amer Board Fam Prac 2000; Vol 13, No. 1, (Jan-Feb).

10. (no author listed). What Lies Ahead for Family Physicians? Fam Pract Management 2000;

11. Stapleton S. Early Screening for Lung Cancer Gains Renewed Interest. Amer Med News 2000; (Jan 17).

12. Jaret P. The Antibiotic Crisis. Hippocrates 1998; (Nov).

13. Klein SA. Federal Judge Upholds Texas Law on HMO Liability. American Medical News 1998; (Oct 12).

About the Author

Philip Caravella, M.D., F.A.A.F.P., was the youngest president of The Cleveland Academy of Family Physicians when elected in 1980. He has been a Fellow of the American Academy of Family Physicians since the early 1980s, and he won the Max Gansloser Award for achievement and research in psychiatry awarded by St. Louis University School of Medicine. He has been a Diplomat of the American Board of Family Practice since 1975.

Dr. Caravella has practiced in many medical arenas, including military medicine, medical education, medical research, medical administration, physician recruitment, solo practice, group practice, and most recently as a full-time family physician with The Cleveland Clinic Foundation, the leading cardiac surgery center in the world.

In 1971, when working at The Cleveland Clinic in the department of hematology-oncology, Dr. Caravella was a member of the team under the direction of Dr. James Hewlitt that performed the first bone marrow transplant in the Midwest.

In his career as a family physician he has treated over 10,000 patients, delivered over 200 babies, assisted over 800 patients in quitting smoking, and is an expert in providing preventive health care services.

Dr. Caravella was at the forefront of family medicine education, becoming the first assistant director of the family medicine residency-training program at Fairview General Hospital in Cleveland, Ohio, during the 1970s. He later directed a family residency program at Riverside Hospital in Toledo, Ohio. He taught for years as an assistant clinical professor both at Case Western Reserve University in Cleveland and at the Medical College of Ohio in Toledo. He is a life member of Who's Who.

Dr. Caravella has experience in providing presentations on a variety of subjects to physicians, medical students, nurses, and the lay public. A local television station also interviewed him in

1998 for the Great American Smoke Out on effective methods of smoking cessation.

In 1980, Dr. Caravella received his favorite honor – one given him by his family practice residents at Fairview Hospital. The residents created an award referred to as the Philip Caravella, M.D. Bedside Clinical Excellence Award – to be given annually to the most deserving resident in family medicine upon graduation.

Dr. Caravella's publications include an article in *The Ohio Family Physicians News* and a commentary in *Critical Issues in Family Practice*.